Mapping Crime In Its Community Setting

Preface to the Internet Edition

The economics of academic publishing are such that books go out of print fairly quickly, long before their useful lifetime has expired. This was the case with Mapping Crime in Its Community Setting, published in 1991 by Springer-Verlag; it predated the emergence of crime mapping as the powerful crime analysis tool it has become. We retrieved the copyright from Springer last year and decided that, rather than republish it in paper, we would put it on the web and make it available for free. The Library of the University of Illinois at Chicago graciously consented to put store the book on its "reading room" site (http://www.uic.edu/depts/lib/forr/).

Publication of our book was followed by the very successful National Institute of Justice program testing crime mapping elsewhere; called the Drug Market Analysis Program (with the apt acronym D-MAP), cities from San Diego to Pittsburgh to Jersey City to Hartford implemented (in San Diego's case, augmented) computerized crime mapping projects that still flourish. It was also the forerunner of the Chicago Police Department's ICAM (Information Collection for Automated Mapping) system, which has been up and running for a half-dozen years.

As its title implies, the book puts computer-based crime mapping in its community context, where "community" refers both to the police community and the neighborhoods they serve. We discuss how it can be used to incorporate a true and sustainable form of community policing, where the police and community organizations form partnerships to provide communities with the support and protection they need. Of course, maintaining a partnership of this nature is difficult, but we feel that it is well worth the effort.

The technological context of this book is now quite dated. This project started five years after IBM introduced its first personal computer, and the Macintosh had been out for only two years. For example, all of our "geocoding" was done by hand, and the data were sent from place to place by "sneaker LAN," that is, by carrying diskettes from site to site. Yet the project's essential findings are still as applicable today as they were ten years ago: crime mapping is an excellent tool for use by police analysts and administrators; its proper implementation requires police organizations to make substantive changes in the way they do business; and it can be used very effectively as a platform for building cooperative relationships between police and communities and for incorporating dynamic mapping and other (non-police) data as a means of understanding the nature of the communities the police serve. As with any tool, it can also be used inappropriately. Great care, for example, must be given to maintaining the confidentiality of the information the database contains, especially concerning people already victimized, and to attend to unintended organizational consequences of tool use. These matters all receive attention in the book.

Although the text replicates the original printed book faithfully, the figures have been scanned in and are not as crisp as we would like. Most readers, however, are familiar with the output of crime mapping software and recognize that the true output is much more readable than these renditions. Moreover, our project predated color

Macs and PCs, let alone color printers. In any event, we hope that this volume provides readers with a historical perspective of the field and introduces them to the promises and problems of computer mapping, both of which persist as this innovation is further implemented in communities across the nation.

Michael D. Maltz   Andrew C. Gordon   Warren Friedman

April 2000

Foreword

The following is the text of a letter written by LeRoy Martin, Superintendent of the Chicago Police Department. It accompanied the report to the National Institute of Justice on which this book is based.

I am pleased to inform you that we have completed our review of "Mapping Crime in Its Community Setting" prepared by Michael D. Maltz of the University of Illinois at Chicago, Andrew C. Gordon of Northwestern University, and Warren Friedman of the Chicago Alliance of Neighborhood Safety. We are pleased that the Chicago Police Department was chosen by the Department of Justice to participate in this effort. Needless to say, the benefits to be derived from the study are attributable to the shared vision and commitment of our police personnel, the academicians and community representatives who participated in these efforts. We feel that we have all learned from this experiment, and are hopeful that the knowledge gained can benefit other police administrators and planners.

We must caution the readers relative to both the purpose and the content of this report. We ask that the readers of this report remain cognizant of the fact that this project was undertaken to determine if the application of computerized technology could enhance the efficiency and effectiveness of police efforts in the community. We suggest that the readers not interpret or construe this report as an analysis of Department policy of operations. Some of the authors' perceptions are not shared by all, and in some cases, the information provided to them informally by individual members of the Department is not completely accurate. Consequently, readers with intimate knowledge of Department policy and procedure would take exception to some of the information contained in this report.

Because of the complexity of this project and the resulting report, we never could expect to resolve every point of disagreement. The authors have, in fact, incorporated many of the Department's suggestions into the report and have made a number of technical corrections to information contained in earlier drafts. Rather than debate perceptions or philosophies, we prefer to endorse the project which we believe was most worthwhile.

We are most grateful for the interest and consideration given to the Chicago Police Department by all those involved in the project. The enthusiasm and spirit of cooperation which evolved from this endeavor will undoubtedly lead to greater cooperation and hopefully greater advances in future projects.

LeRoy Martin
Superintendent
Chicago Police Department
December 18, 1989

Preface

The research project, "Mapping Crime in Its Community Setting," grew out of a series of concerns. The primary concerns, of course, were the safety of the community and finding ways to improve it. The project was also geared to be responsive to developments in technology, to recent findings about problem-oriented policing, and to the development of an environments in which a long-term partnership could be forged among the participants. All of the institutional partners in the project–the Chicago Police Department, two universities, and a consortium of community organizations–were active participants in the development of the project; no preplanned research design was imposed on the project by a research expert. Because the goal of the project was to develop a crime mapping system in which all groups were to participate, we felt it important that all should participate in deciding its direction as well.

The level of active participation in the design and implementation of the project enriched and complicated the project in many ways. One consequence of the obvious and immediate utility of the mapping tools was that we were required simultaneously to develop the system and to study what we developed, how we developed it, and the uses to which it was put–all while we were modifying it and attempting to train others to use it. We were learning about each other's capacities and shortcomings at the same time. In other words, the project was implemented on many different levels at the same time. Because it was unexpectedly put to immediate daily use, we found ourselves becoming immersed in day-to-day detail, designing computer crime screens, making and modifying maps and report forms, setting up and modifying distribution systems, distributing maps, going out into the field and getting feedback, training people to use the computer, gathering data from the community, and responding to requests from other police districts and from detectives for mapping assistance. Thus, how the project was implemented was, we believe, as important to the success of the project as were the specific project elements.

The project concerned itself with the development and implementation of a computer-assisted crime analysis strategy called Microcomputer-Assisted Police Analysis and Deployment System (MAPADS) for police and community groups. This volume focuses both on the mapping system itself and on the social and organizational context in which the mapping system evolved. Going beyond a mere technical description is important for several reasons. First, police departments differ considerably from city to city. Second, the state of community organization also differs from city to city. Furthermore, relations between the police and communities are always complicated. In light of this, we felt it important to describe the social context in which this research was conducted in order to give readers an appreciation of the relevance of our approach to their own situations.

This volume describes the mapping system's characteristics and performance in enough detail to permit others to determine its usefulness for their own situations. Our emphasis has been on facilitating rather than on replacing the analytic capacities of knowledgeable crime analysts and on assessing other ways in which graphics-oriented data presentation–and analytic strategies appropriate to such data–might enhance the crime fighting efforts of police and concerned citizens.

The project design was based on a number of principles (see Chapter 3). First, we felt that a computer is more appropriately used for crime analysis as a "power steering" device, where the computer provides the power but the person does the steering, rather than as an "autopilot" device where the computer (or whoever programmed it) takes over all of the functions of the person. Second, we felt that statistical analysis has many limitations for analysis of crime data and that the best analytic tool is the individual who searches through the data to find patterns that would not readily be apparent statistically; the computer was to be used to make it easier to spot the patterns and to augment the analyst's memory. Third, we felt that the best way to develop the system was to work directly in conjunction with the users so that they could determine what kind of data they wanted to be presented and how they wanted it presented.

The project produced a number of useful and unexpected findings. While graphical techniques are hardly new to police work–crime maps have probably existed as long as the police have–their automation caused them to have much greater utility. In particular, we noted their impact in the following areas in the units in which it was implemented: in combining data from different sources (see Chapter 6); in providing an "institutional memory" of a beat (see Chapter 6); in providing detectives with the ability to search for patterns more readily (see Chapter 7); in permitting "proactive management" by the district commander (see Chapter 8); and in improving community relations between the police and community organizations (see Chapters 9 and 10). In addition, we felt that utilization would have been even greater had we provided patrol officers with more (and more relevant) training (see Chapter 11). These areas are summarized below.

Combining Data

One of the drawbacks of incident-driven policing and specialization by crime type is that officers working on different crimes and/or crime types do not get a chance to compare notes; in large cities, there is just too much going on to do so. When we plotted burglary data on the same map on which we superimposed a narcotics "hot spot" (provided to the CPD by community residents). we noticed a striking correlation (see Chapter 6, Figure 6.10). Thus, the crime analyst can combine data from different sources (not just crime data, but perhaps also calls-for-service data and other data as well–see Chapter 12) on the maps and infer different patterns from them.

Institutional Memory

This ability to combine data can be understood more readily by realizing that the maps can serve as a beat's (or district's) institutional memory. That is, the maps are the only place where one can see everything that is going on in an area. As we explain, patrol officers cannot know everything happening on their beats–they are there for only five shifts a week and cannot even be expected to remember everything that happened during those five shifts. Only on a map can the entire beat experience be put together and the pattern discerned from the individual incidents.

Detectives

Implementation of the system in a field detective unit proved instructive in terms of how such a system could best be used by detectives. First, detectives need to read case report narratives to get a feel for the incident. However, they normally abstract only a few points from each narrative; they enter this information into the data base themselves because it is an interpretive function that they feel can only be done by experienced detectives. Second, the integrative aspect of computer-combined data helps to overcome one of the most counterproductive aspects of detective work, lack of sharing of information. Just as the computer serves as a beat's institutional memory, it can also serve as an integrator of information about different offenders and different cases, that is, input by different detectives on case and supplementary reports. Third, issues relating to the reward structure may have an impact on MAPADS implementation. The reward structure of most police departments is perceived to be heavily biased toward the number of arrests made by officers, producing a significant impediment to the sharing of relevant information, particularly between detectives and tactical officers. Behavior that is irrational from the point of view of the department (information hoarding) may be rational from the perspective of individual officers (career building), and it is important that any new information strategy respond to these realities.

Proactive Management

The timeliness of the data and the accessibility and "user-friendliness" of the system permitted the district commander to make decisions about deployment of tactical units and directed patrol missions based on current and readily absorbed information. In essence, it freed him from the handcuffs of a cumbersome and unresponsive data system, permitting him to target developing problems. By his own report, the central computer system was so difficult to use, required so much paperwork, and was so likely to result in out-of-date information that he was reluctant to make requests for information. The locally available mapping and data system made it far easier to make specialized requests, to ask last-minute questions, and to follow upon earlier queries. The result was a range of innovative, data-driven activity that had never previously been possible, including beat-level productivity measures; specialized narcotics activity, crime awareness, and gang activity bulletins based on mapped data; tailored reports and maps for beat, officers and for directed patrol missions; and informed presentations for concerned citizens that resulted in more productive and cooperative meetings.

Police-Community Relations

The two-way exchange of information between the police department and community organizations was one of the most significant contributions of this crime mapping project–one with implications vastly beyond the project itself. This aspect inevitably suffered from starting inertia: Neither the police nor the community organizations had much prior experience with hands-on computer use, although CANS had some months of experience providing computer maps to member organizations. The project was designed so that the maps would be coproduced by the police and the community representatives, embedding cooperation in the process. Police officers grew in their appreciation of the value of the community's perceptions and of the information citizens could provide.

The accidental timing of interactions that were perceived as successful by both sides was probably quite important. In one instance, the police thought that residents' fear of crime had overcome their objectivity and that their alleging that one busy corner was especially dangerous (particularly on weekends) was a clear error. But long-term data for the area, which community analysts were able to provide, and calls-for-service data, which were added to the mapped analysis, verified the accuracy of the residents' perceptions; relying on crime statistics alone gave a misleading picture of the corner's problems. This experience resulted in a vigorous response by the district commander, and each party's respect for the other was solidified.

These experiences, combined with the current (and we feel appropriate) development of problem-oriented policing strategies, have led us to conclude that a partnership can and should be developed and maintained between community organizations and the police–not just with respect to community tensions, as has always been the case, but with respect to fostering a working relationship that focuses on crime as an interest of mutual concern.

Training

Among police users of MAPADS, the tactical patrol unit, the detectives, and the district administration found the tools to be immediately useful; however, most patrol officers found it to be a waste of time. This was due partly to the inadequacy of the training we provided for patrol officers, partly to the limitations of the software, partly to the ethic of patrol officers, and partly to fundamental differences in the utility of such systems for various people with various responsibilities. In any case, we feel that a police department should develop a training program prior to full implementation of MAPADS. Officers should be instructed in types of patterns to look for, how to obtain special maps for their own use, what types of information can be combined, and other aspects of the system. If this information is provided to beat officers, they will be better able to perform their jobs and will do so with a greater awareness of the beat's activity patterns and potential problems.

Acknowledgments

The research for the crime mapping project owes its existence and support to a number of individuals in the National Institute of Justice (NIJ) and the Chicago Police Department (CPD). The crime mapping project was supported by NIJ Grant 86-IJ-CX-0074 and by a generous donation of equipment from Apple Computer, Inc. During the project's lifetime we received a great deal of encouragement from George Shollenberger and Fred Heinzelmann of NIJ. Within the CPD, the overall support the crime mapping project has received has been excellent; both Fred Rice, who retired in 1988 as superintendent of police, and LeRoy Martin, the current superintendent of police, gave this project support from the top, support that encouraged us and permitted us to work freely in the department.

The project itself was jointly conceived by a number of individuals. In the early 1980s, Michael Maltz, the project director at the University of Illinois at Chicago, had been working with Dennis Nowicki, then deputy superintendent of administrative services and now chief of police in Joliet. Illinois, on a proposal (unsuccessful) to NIJ to develop a crime mapping system. At the same time, Warren Friedman and Andrew Gordon, the Chicago Alliance for Neighborhood Safety and Northwestern University project directors, respectively, who had been working with computerized mapping of crime for community purposes. asked the CPD to provide them with crime data. Chief Nowicki suggested that we work with each other, and this project is the result of our joining forces.

Another former CPD official, John Jemilo, who recently retired as first deputy superintendent and is currently executive director of the Chicago Crime Commission, was instrumental in promoting the crime mapping project within the CPD. Long an administrator who believed in a strong community role in policing, Jemilo had been attempting to lay the groundwork for a pilot police district, one that would do what pilots are supposed to do–lead the way in the implementation of innovative policing. When the possibility of this project came up, Jemilo sat down with the project codirectors and hammered out an agreement that formed the basis for the crime mapping project.

Sergeant Robert Lombardo, then executive assistant to the first deputy superintendent and currently commanding officer of the Asset Forfeiture Unit of the Organized Crime Division, was invaluable in the day-to-day operation of the project. Not only did he insure that bureaucratic problems were minimized, but he also was involved in the substantive aspects of the research, especially with respect to the neighborhood and community orientation of crime and policing.

The late Ronald Manka, director of the CPD Data Systems Division, was also of great help to us. He made sure that we were able to obtain the information that we requested and was instrumental in the CPD's plans to implement the crime mapping system citywide.

Matt Rodriguez, deputy superintendent of technical services, supported our efforts and has been working with the project team to develop the criteria for a citywide system. He has also been a driving force behind the CPD's efforts to improve and upgrade its emergency response and dispatching systems.

This support from headquarters personnel made our task much easier. But our task was made possible, enjoyable, and fruitful by those who were involved in it with us on a daily basis. In District 25, Commander Matthias E. Casey (now deputy chief of the Detective Division-Administration) and police officer Marc Buslik (now in the Data Systems Division) became the resident experts in crime mapping, showing us what could be done when a dedicated administrator and an innovative tactical officer were released from the handcuffs of an antiquated data system and given the tools to permit patrol resources to be allocated when and where they were needed–almost on a daily basis. They far exceeded our expectations for police operational resources. Additionally, Officer Buslik provided invaluable assistance in the preparation of this book. We found the same reception when we involved the Area 5 Detective Division in the crime mapping project, from police sergeant George Parich and detective Chris Alberts; they took the lead and we followed.

We received a great deal of value in our interactions with John Firman, Carolyn Rebecca Block, and James Spring of the Illinois Criminal Justice Information Authority and from Glenn Pierce of Northeastern University. Sergeant Maurice McGough of the St. Petersburg Police Department and Lieutenant David Doan of the Los Angeles Police Department provided us with a perspective from other operating agencies. Two anonymous NIJ reviewers gave this book careful and helpful scrutiny. A number of CPD officials provided us with critical review as well. In addition, there are a great many other CPD officials whose assistance and support should be acknowledged. Many of these individuals are not mentioned by name, but their use of MAPADS is represented in this report in various ways. We were fortunate to have such a receptive department in which to develop and implement the crime mapping concept.

This book is a joint effort of the principal investigators as well as others, including both colleagues and graduate students. Although authorship is difficult to attribute because the book went through many drafts, all of which were reviewed by the principal investigators, we do wish to give credit to the individuals whose work is represented in this report–credit for authorship is as important to academics as credit for arrests is to police officers. Primary authorship for each chapter is as follows:

Chapter 1: Michael D. Maltz, Warren Friedman, and Andrew C. Gordon
Chapter 2: Michael D. Maltz, Andrew C. Gordon, and Warren Friedman
Chapters 3-5: Andrew C. Gordon and Michael D. Maltz

Chapter 6: Michael D. Maltz and Douglas R. Thomson
Chapter 7: John P. Walsh
Chapter 8: Michael D. Maltz
Chapter 9: Paul Schnorr, Andrew C. Gordon, and Warren Friedman
Chapter 10: Warren Friedman
Chapter 11: Douglas R. Thomson
Chapter 12: Michael D. Maltz
Chapter 13: John P. Walsh and Michael D. Maltz
Appendix B: Robert K. LeBailley and Andrew C. Gordon
Appendix D: Marc Buslik

Contents

Glossary

AREA   A geographic unit within the CPD, consisting of three to five patrol districts.

ALGORITHM   A set of rules to follow, such as in a computer program, or a list of steps to take.

BEAT   A geographic unit within a police district; the responsibility of the officer(s) assigned to patrolling it.

CAD Computer-aided dispatch.

CANS   Chicago Alliance for Neighborhood Safety. a consortium of community organizations concerned with community safety and one of the partners in the crime mapping project.

CAO   Crime analysis officer, a role that was created within District 25 of the CPD specifically for the crime mapping project.

CAU Crime Analysis Unit, the unit in the CPD's Detective Division charged with the mission of generating crime patterns and information bulletins.

CFS   Calls for service, calls that are originated by citizens' calling the police. usually over the 911 emergency telephone system.

CGA   Color graphics adapter. referring to the plug-in card and monitor for a personal computer that permits the display of color graphics as output from the computer.

CMS   Case management sergeant, the detective in an area responsible for assigning cases to detectives.

CIN   Chicago Intervention Network, a community-based, city-sponsored organization that deals on a grass-roots level with community safety problems.

CLEARANCE   The clearing up of a crime, usually (but not necessarily) on the basis of an arrest.

CPD   Chicago Police Department, the department in which the crime mapping project was carried out and one of the partners in the project.

CRIME PATTERN   A term used by the CPD to denote a collection of crimes that point to the characteristics of a particular perpetrator(s); for example, physical appearance, dress, or behaviors repeated in committing crimes.

CRIMES An acronym for Case Report Information and Management Evaluation

System; it is a data base that contains all case reports.

DBMS   Data base management system, a computer program (i.e., a software product) used to store, manipulate, and analyze data.

DOWNLOAD   To copy a computer file or data set from a mainframe computer (or computer tape) to a personal computer (or to a PC diskette).

DIRECTED PATROL MISSION A patrol assignment given to beat and/or tactical officers to pay specific attention to a location (e.g., a hot spot), a group (e.g., a gang), or a pattern of activity (e.g., open garage doors).

DISTRICT   A patrol unit within the CPD, one of 25 within the city of Chicago.

EGA Extended graphics adapter, referring to the plug-in card and monitor for a personal computer that permits the display of high-resolution color graphics as output from the computer.

HOT SPOT A location where a number of criminal incidents have taken place or where the community sees a certain danger even though criminal incidents may not have been recorded by the police; in other words, the community and/or police perceive a chronic safety problem at this location.

ICJIA   Illinois Criminal Justice Information Authority.

INDEX CRIME A crime appearing on the Index of Crime published by the U.S. Federal Bureau of Investigation; these crimes were selected for their seriousness and because they were considered to be most likely to be reported to the police: murder, rape, aggravated assault, robbery, burglary, auto theft, larceny, and arson.

INFORMATION BULLETIN   A term used by the CPD to denote patterns that identify a type of crime and a geographical. pattern, but may contain little information about the offenders.

LAPD   Los Angeles Police Department.

LEADS   Law Enforcement Agencies Data System, a system containing a database of wanted persons or vehicles within Illinois that provides interconnection to other law enforcement databases such as the Illinois Secretary of State System (drivers licenses, motor vehicles) the National Law Enforcement Telecommunication System (NLETS) and the FBI's National Crime Information Center (NCIC).

MAINFRAME   A large computer that can accommodate many users at the same time and that can store, retrieve, and analyze a great deal of data.

MAPADS Microcomputer-Assisted Police Analysis and Deployment System, the system developed and studied in the crime mapping research project.

MO Modus operandi (Latin for method of operation), the characteristic "signature" of an offender, the pattern he or she normally uses when committing a crime.

MODEM An acronym for MOdulator-DEModulator, an electronic device that converts data (in this case, sequences of computer bits) into signals that can be sent over telephone lines, and vice versa.

MS-DOS Microsoft Disk Operating System, referring to the operating software used by IBM personal computers and compatibles.

NIJ National Institute of Justice, the research arm of the U.S. Department of Justice.

NU Northwestern University, whose Center for Urban Affairs and Policy Research is one of the partners in the crime mapping project.

PART I CRIME Essentially the same as Index crime; the more serious crimes reported by police departments to the F.B.I.

PC Personal computer.

PISTOL Paperless Information System Totally On-Line, a system developed by the St. Petersburg (FL) Police Department to permit case reports to be written directly into hand-held portable computers provided to patrol officers.

PROBLEM-ORIENTED POLICING A strategy of policing that focuses on the underlying problems that generate criminal incidents rather than focusing only on each individual incident as it arises.

RAMIS A data base management system used by the CPD on its mainframe computer.

RECAP Repeat Complaint Address Policing, a program that focuses on the few locations that generate a very high number of calls for police service.

REVIEW OFFICER The officer charged with reviewing case reports generated by patrol officers, filing and maintaining these reports, and preparing the 24-Hour Activity Report for the district commander.

SAS Statistical Analysis System, a DBMS software package available for mainframe and personal computers.

SES Socioeconomic status.

SPSS Statistical Package for the Social Sciences, a DBMS software package available for mainframe and personal computers.

STAC Spatial and Temporal Analysis of Crime, a geographically based crime analysis system developed by ICJIA.

TAC UNIT   The tactical unit of a district, which has district-wide responsibility for directed patrol missions against crime; tac officers usually are in plain clothes.

THROUGHPUT The rate of transmission of data.

24-HOUR ACTIVITY REPORT   A report, based on case reports filed by patrol officers, that describes criminal occurrences within a district over the past 24 hours.

UIC University of Illinois at Chicago, whose Center for Research in Law and Justice is one of the partners in the crime mapping project.

UCPP   Urban Crime Prevention Program, an early community-based crime prevention program of the Law Enforcement Assistance Administration.

VGA Video graphics adapter, referring to the plug-in card and monitor for a personal computer that permits the display of very high-resolution color graphics as output from the computer.

Introduction

This volume is concerned with the use of statistics in a law enforcement context. Statistics does not just deal with numbers. It is concerned with making sense of data of all sorts and with trying to find patterns that may be hidden in data.

Many of the standard statistical techniques used to find patterns require the analyst to have some prior knowledge about the characteristics of the data. For example, a favorite assumption made by statisticians and social scientists is that the data are normally distributed.

Making such assumptions is not the only way to uncover patterns, nor is it necessarily the best way, particularly when the assumptions are violated (which they are more frequently than many would care to admit). This is especially true about the data we deal with in this volume–offense data. They are generated by hundreds of individual offenders, each of whom may be individually patternable but when analyzed together appear to be completely random and unpatternable.

Individual analysts who have studied offender behavior may be able to select a number of offenses that appear to have been committed by the same offender and may attempt to analyze that individual's offense patterns. But they do not use statistical algorithms to do so. Imagine the fate of the crime analyst who tells his superior, "I'm sorry, but I can't analyze this series of rapes. We only have three cases, so we can't get statistical significance."

Most standard statistical methods are inapplicable for crime analysis for another reason. For the most part, these methods are used primarily to *test* hypotheses. In the exploratory data analysis engaged in by the police, the goal is to *generate* hypotheses regarding who might have committed these crimes and what they might do next.

One of the best pattern recognition devices known to humanity is the human mind, especially when the data are visual. Although the brain may not be as good as a statistical algorithm for finding patterns in *numerical* data, it is incomparable for finding patterns in *visual* data. And crime data can–and, we believe, should be put in a geographical (i.e., visual) context in order for analysts to make the most sense out of them. In that vein, the research described in this volume can best be summarized by the aphorism "One picture is worth a thousand words." Our goal during the crime mapping project was to present the crime data to analysts in a form that made it easier for them to infer patterns and trends.

Of course, algorithms can also help analysts find patterns of a geographical nature. It is certainly possible to write a computer program to analyze data geographically; for example, to investigate the relationship between the robbery of fast food outlets and expressway entrances, or between garage burglaries and nearby drug activity, or between purse snatchings and mass transit routes. But this would overload a system with algorithms that are useless 99% of the time. It is more appropriate–and effective–to present the data in such a way that a canny police officer can do the job.

The effort we report on in this volume is the continuation and extension of a trend found in dealing with information in fields other than law enforcement–that is, concern with information processing in the global sense. Over the past few decades we have seen data processing technology and procedures move from focusing almost entirely on numerical data processing (numbers as data) to embracing text processing (words and characters as data) as a major component. More recently, as computer power has been diffused throughout the country, with the video screen instead of paper as the primary output medium, graphics and image processing (pictures as data) have grown in importance. In this volume we show how to capitalize on this trend in a police setting.

We also describe how the crime mapping project was conceived and implemented. A research project of this nature does not spring up full-blown out of thin air. It takes a great deal of planning, arguing, proposing and rejecting of ideas, succeeding, and failing. In other words, the context of this research is, we feel, an integral part of the effort and one that should be described in order to provide a clear understanding of its goals and accomplishments.

This volume describes the goals and accomplishments of the research project, "Mapping Crime in Its Community Setting," which was funded by a grant from the National Institute of Justice to the CPD and its subgrantees, the Chicago Alliance for Neighborhood Safety, the Center for Urban Affairs and Policy Research at Northwestern University, and the Center for Research in Law and Justice at the University of Illinois at Chicago. It was also assisted by a generous donation of computer equipment and software from Apple Computer, Inc. The project began on November 1, 1986, and ended on September 30, 1988.

The purpose of the grant was, broadly, to implement a computer-based crime mapping system in a patrol unit and in a detective unit of the CPD and determine its effectiveness as a tool for law enforcement and in enhancing police cooperation and communication with community organizations. Because the implementation and the assessment of its utility were to be conducted simultaneously, the evaluation was not expected to be rigorous and formal but rather descriptive, indicating what such a mapping system might be able to do in a police department. Therefore, those who are expecting a formal evaluation of crime mapping as implemented in the CPD, with experimental and control groups and random assignment, will have to wait a bit longer. This volume describes the system's implementation and its use, and discusses some of the broader issues raised by the project.

This volume is comprised of three parts: Part 1, entitled "The Mapping Project and Information," describes the crime mapping project's origins and participants; the technical, administrative, and historical context of the project; the way in which information is currently used in police departments for crime analysis; the nature of community perceptions of safety and information concerning incivilities; and the project's goals and objectives.

Part II, entitled "Using the Maps," describes the manner in which the units within the CPD were selected for implementation; the manner in which the system was used for managerial purposes by the CPD; the way detectives used the system; how patrol officers responded to the system; and the effectiveness of the system in promoting police-community cooperation in the joint provision of and use of crime and community-generated data.

Part III, entitled "Implications of this Project," looks to the ways in which this project could be enhanced–by institutionalizing cooperation between the police and community organizations concerning crime analysis and patrol policies; by improving training to facilitate the use of maps by police; by incorporation of different types of data on the maps; and by considering the role of computers in improving communication within police departments.

Part I
The Mapping Project and Information

During the summer of 1988, Patrol officers Barry Eichner and Edward Carfora of District 25 were assigned the responsibility of preliminary investigations of incidents involving racial and ethnic tension. These events do not occur frequently, so the district commander decided to have them spend their time on proactive patrol activity as well. They met with the district's crime analysis officer, looking for specific criminal activity in the geographic areas where the racial/ethnic incidents had taken place. The crime analysis officer immediately pulled up maps on the microcomputer screen that showed crime occurrences in these areas during the month of June. After looking the maps over, the officers noticed a pattern in the occurrence and recovery of stolen vehicles; Many of the vehicles were stolen from a small area on one beat (Fig. I.1) and recovered in a small area on another beat (Fig. 1.2). The officers requested and were given copies of the maps displaying the locations of stolen vehicles and recovered stolen vehicles, as well as details of the incidents displayed on the maps (Figs. I.3 and I.4). Although the officers had not been patrolling the areas displayed on the maps previously, they were able to familiarize themselves with the area and come up to speed more quickly by having the maps augment the listing of incidents.

The officers felt that the offenders would probably continue to work those areas. Based on the maps, the officers developed a strategy for the areas, determining when and where the offenders might be likely to steal cars and dispose of the stripped vehicles. The officers then began a surveillance of the areas during the course of their normal investigative activities, and subsequently arrested a group of offenders in an auto theft ring, clearing up nine auto thefts.

The officers requested follow-up maps as well. The subsequent maps showed increased auto theft activity in other areas, so they revised their patrolling strategies to reflect the changes. Thus, they were able to continue tracking the activity throughout the district.

Approximately 6 weeks later, again in an area of high car theft activity (according to the maps), the officers arrested one of the same offenders along with two new offenders and cleared additional auto thefts and several burglaries. Two days later, while patrolling the area targeted with the help of the maps, they arrested another one of the first group of offenders and cleared two other auto thefts. All of this arrest activity would not have been possible had the area not been pinpointed by the original map and tracked by subsequent follow-up maps. On July 18, 1989, the officers received a departmental commendation for this and subsequent map-based proactive efforts.

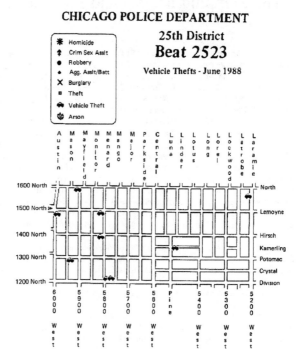

Figure I.1. Computer map showing vehicle thefts in one beat

CHICAGO POLICE DEPARTMENT

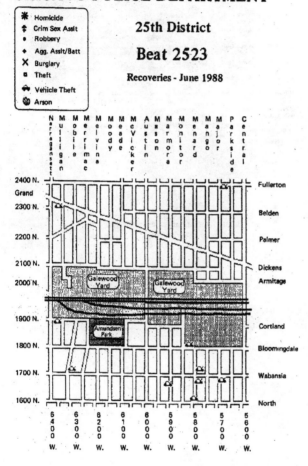

Homicide
Crim Sex Asslt
Robbery
Agg. Asslt/Batt
Burglary
Theft
Vehicle Theft
Arson

25th District

Beat 2523

Recoveries - June 1988

Figure I.2. Computer map showing recoveries
of stolen vehicles in one beat

When	What	Where	Who & What
88/06/08 0430 /	Vehicle Theft	15 -- Laramie [2623] K 232783	MR3757 ILL 88 Offender Known. 1976 Buick Regal Yellow in color.
2300 / 2300	Vehicle Theft Attempt	12 -- Mason K 235208	1981 Olds Cutlass Attempt on V
88/06/13 0230 /	Vehicle Theft	15 -- Mayfield K 240864	CC 4430 ILL 88 75 Chev Monte Carlo 2dr White & brown
88/06/17 Unk	Vehicle Theft	58 -- Hirsch K 250273	License number unknown 76 Olds Cutlass 2dr green
88/06/19 9040 /	Vehicle Theft	67 -- Dickstor K 251021	KH 5230 ILL 88 79 Dodge Omni Hatchback Gray
1100 /	Vehicle Theft	14 -- Menard K 249760	9TV 3305 NC 89 86 Toyota MR 2 2dr Red
88/06/20 2200 / 0415	Vehicle Theft	15 -- Menard K 253085	FM 2244 ILL 88 84 Chev Gamin - window van. Brown and gold
88/06/22 0001 / 0500	Vehicle Theft	54 -- Kumshing K 268996	DOG238 ILL 88 1982 Buick Regal White in color
0500 / 0700	Vehicle Theft Recovery	67 -- Division K 256995	LWD 182 ILL 89 1976 Chev. wagon Gray in color

Beat of Occurrence Count: 9

Overall Count: 9

Figure I.3. Computer-generated lists giving
details of vehicle thefts shown on map.

2513	88/06/03	0400	63-- Grand		79	Chev	Monte	2dr
2513	88/06/05	1620	63-- Cortland		81	Buick	Lesabre	4dr
2513	88/06/06	2100	17-- Mobile		82	Buick		2dr
2513	88/06/10	1900	16-- Marmora		87	Olds	Cutlass	2dr
2513	88/06/12	1340	58-- Bloomingdale		83	Buick		4dr
2513	88/06/13	0730	16-- Menard		82	Chrysler	New Yorker	4dr
2513	88/06/15	1630	16-- Menard		76	Buick	Regal	2dr
2513	88/06/19	1400	17-- Menard		75	Olds	Cutlass	2dr
2513	88/06/20	0430	16-- Major		81	Olds	Cutlass	2dr
2513	88/06/26	0500	56-- Fullerton		82	Buick	Regal	2dr

Figure I.4 Computer-generated list giving
details of vehicle recoveries shown on map.

CHAPTER 1

The Context of the Mapping Project

In this chapter we describe the context in which the project "Mapping Crime in Its Community Context" was developed. Because the focal point of the project is information about crime and public safety, we first discuss how information about crime, which generally comes from the community, is handled in a police department. In the crime mapping project the CPD was the grantee and CANS, a consortium of 10 community organizations, was one of the three subgrantees. A historical perspective is given of the relationship between these two organizations and of their relationship to the two other subgrantees, Northwestern University and the University of Illinois at Chicago.

Although the enhancement of communication between the police and community groups was certainly accomplished during the crime mapping project, it was not the project's primary goal. The goal was to determine the manner in which crime analysis activity, both within the CPD and by community organizations, might be improved through the use of crime maps. The project's goals are described in this chapter, as are their relevance to the concerns of the National Institute of Justice.

The crime mapping project focused on how information about crime is used, by both the police and community organizations, which are both involved in the processing of crime information. Normally, the first indication that a crime has occurred is a call from a community resident to the police. The police then handle this information in different ways and use it as a basis for allocating resources, but ordinarily the police do not provide the community with any additional information about the way they are handling this crime or others. In some cases, this is a cause of friction between the police and the community.

This chapter deals with some of these issues. It discusses the nature of crime information; the relationship between the police and community organizations in Chicago, and between the CPD and university researchers as well; and effects these relationships had on the manner in which the participants conceptualized and developed the crime mapping project.

Information

Information is the lifeblood of the police. It is used to determine how to allocate patrol resources among districts and among beats within districts, when and where to patrol, who the likely suspects of a crime are, which offenses are likely to be solved, and in general how to serve and protect the community. For the most part, this information is provided to the police from community residents, who call the police and expect an appropriate response from them. The relationship between the police and the community, therefore, is a key aspect of its ability to provide for the safety and well-being of that community. This reliance on information from the community raises a number of important questions summarized by Kelling (1978) as follows:

How can we improve the quality and quantity of police-citizen contacts so that citizens report more crime, give police information–both formally and informally–about crime patterns, and discuss community concerns? How can we improve the ability of the individual police officer and the organization to gather that information, store it, and bring it to bear on appropriate events and issues? How can we improve the police officer's and the police organization's ability to understand their community so that they can better interpret the information they receive? (p. 180)

Information relevant to public safety and security originates from a number of sources both within and outside a police department. When a citizen's call comes in on the 911 emergency telephone lines[1] a dispatch card is filled out and a patrol car is dispatched based on that information. The information on the card is keyed into a computer for storage on a data tape and the cards themselves are kept for a year before being archived. The telephone and radio communications are also stored on an audio tape, although for a shorter period of time, so that a specific incident can be traced from its inception if the circumstances warrant.

If the incident requires a report, the responding officer fills one out, and information from that report gets entered into a computer data base for later analysis. Photocopies of the report are disseminated to a number of different units within the police department, the specific unit(s) depending on the nature and location of the incident. This process is described in greater detail in Chapter 2.

Information, therefore, is ubiquitous within a police department. A great deal is collected, not just about criminal incidents. Because any action of the police may be involved in a court proceeding, reports are made on just about everything police

officers do. Utilization of the information, however, is limited compared to the

---

[1]The 911 emergency telephone system is also used for fire and ambulance calls, both of which are handled by the Chicago Fire Department. When these calls come in, they are fast-forwarded to the Chicago Fire Department; the police call-taker (usually a civilian dispatcher aide) stays on the line, however, to make sure the call is completed and to see if police support is needed. In this volume we refer only to the 911 system's use for police emergencies.

amount collected. Much of it serves as a backup to be made available if needed. Although individual case reports are used by the detectives assigned to follow up on a case, the primary use of crime information in its aggregate form is for statistical purposes–to provide information for obtaining district-by-district crime rates or for the FBI's Uniform Crime Reports (UCRs). Very little use is made of the information available on the radio dispatch cards. Although it is true that information is the lifeblood of the police, the blood seems to be circulating very slowly. Also, very little of this information is returned to the public in a usable form.

In a large measure, the information about crime that has been available for public consumption has come from summary reports such as the UCRs, from meetings between the police and concerned community organizations, and from newspapers. Although the summary reports are useful as a general barometer of public safety, they are not specific enough to address community members' concerns about their own neighborhoods nor to serve as a basis for informed community action. The police and the community may have differences in perception about community safety, with police statistics demonstrating the relative safety of the community and residents complaining about the dangerousness of the community despite the police statistics. Newspaper reports are often quite factual because their source is usually the police department; a number of local and neighborhood newspapers have crime columns in which summaries of crimes occurring during the past day or week are provided. However, when a particularly serious or heinous crime occurs, it is given a great deal of play, and crime and police protection often become political footballs.

Word of mouth is another means by which the community receives information about local crime. This is often incomplete and misleading. In some cases some people do. not want their neighbors to know that they have been victimized. In other cases the entire community may find out about a particular crime and, after hearing it from and discussing it with many of their neighbors, may unduly elevate their own sense of insecurity. An interesting example of this occurred to one member of the project staff. A particular crime was related to his entire neighborhood by the school crossing guard, who had contact with virtually the entire community. The result was that the community thought there was a mini-crime wave.

Thus, for the most part, community residents have limited access to crime information, and what information they do receive may be distorted in terms of its actual dangerousness to them, either by its being magnified out of proportion or buried by embarrassed victims. A major purpose of the crime mapping project was to provide a mechanism for greater and more effective utilization of actual information by both the police and community organizations.

Project Participants

The crime mapping project was funded by NIJ starting in November 1986. "Mapping Crime in Its Community Setting" is a title with an important and intended double meaning. *Community setting* refers both to the data on the map and the information that supports it and to the social and organizational context in which the creation and the use of the maps becomes meaningful and productive. The goal of the project was to improve the crime analysis capabilities of police and community organizations by developing a computer-based mapping system. The four organizations involved in the project have expertise in complementary areas of importance to the success of the project, which can be described as follows:

- Chicago Alliance for Neighborhood Safety (CANS): Developing community crime prevention programs and strategies, developing training programs for citizens in these areas, coordinating with police on crime prevention, using police-provided crime data to produce crime maps for community crime prevention, and encouraging volunteer efforts for crime prevention.
- Chicago Police Department (CPD): Crime data collection, crime data quality control procedures, crime pattern analysis, deployment strategies for crime prevention and offender apprehension, and neighborhood involvement through the Beat Representative Program and neighborhood relations officers.
- Northwestern University, Center for Urban Affairs and Policy Research (NU): Working with community groups on crime prevention, developing crime and incivility maps, integrating mapping software into operating agencies and community groups, and investigating the nature of community fear of crime and incivilities.
- University of Illinois at Chicago, Center for Research in Law and Justice (UIC): Developing analytic techniques for studying crime data, conducting research on community responses to crime, conducting research on police information systems and communications procedures, and designing and conducting evaluations of crime control projects.

The four organizations started laying the groundwork for the crime mapping project in September 1985, and thus worked together on it for three years.

Historical Perspective

There is always a measure of difficulty in getting a number of different organizations to work together. When the organizations are as different in aims and philosophies as a police department, a consortium of community organizations, and two universities, the task becomes more difficult. It is further compounded when the prior relationships among the organizations, particularly (but not exclusively) between the CPD and some Chicago community organizations, were less than cordial; as in many cities, they did not start out on the friendliest of terms.

However, in this case these organizations also had a history of constructive interaction on which to build. Although police and community organizations have different agendas, there is also enough overlap to provide the basis for cooperation. In this section, we will elaborate on some of these differences, and discuss the historical development of ties between the various organizations that provided the groundwork for the crime mapping project.

Patrol officers have generally been incident-driven; that is, they have spent most of their time responding to calls for service that originate from the 911 emergency telephone system. In attempting to deal expeditiously with these incidents, they have frequently felt distracted from their duties by the community's concerns, especially when the community's concerns do not relate to "real crime" (i.e., felonies). In return, the police have felt the wrath of community groups and residents, angry at what they perceived as insensitivity to their needs.[2]

In large part, this distrust may have been structurally shaped by the car-bound officer's job definition and the incident-driven policing strategy that determined it. Summoned by calls to 911, to yet another of the approximately 2.2 million incidents to which Chicago police are dispatched each year, police officers can see the neighborhood as a blur. Moreover, an officer may not be racing to a "hot" call but to a minor, noncriminal event, important to the caller but marginal or irrelevant to combatting crime, which is perceived by most patrol officers to be the primary mission of the police. Having finished the call, the officer may remain totally ignorant of the outcome of his or her actions and cynical toward a public that would use valuable police time and resources for such apparent trivia. Under such an incident-driven strategy, responsiveness to community concerns is unsystematic and unsustained.

Another factor that can lead to differences between the police and the community is the fact that police work is measured through solved crimes, not prevented crimes–a reactive rather than a proactive stance. Police officers may not be seen as effective if they make it a practice to find out where crimes are likely to occur, patrol in that area, and thereby discourage crimes. Officers often get recognized for their arrest productivity,[3] although the officer who prevents crime may be of more value to the community. Measuring crimes prevented is not always possible, and attributing crime reduction to a specific police officer is rarely possible, whereas making an arrest is a tangible, measurable work product, attributable to a specific person or persons. The fact that an arrest is a measurable work product and a crime prevented is not means that some supervisors may tend to play it safe by relying on arrest statistics for evaluating officers rather than running the risk of being accused of favoritism by basing evaluations on unmeasurable criteria. This point is further discussed in Chapter 7.

Thus, incident-driven policing and a reactive strategy had created structural problems for police-community communication, but other factors contributed as well. In Chicago, as elsewhere, the relationship was exacerbated by stories in the media of police corruption, troubled relations with minorities, spying on community

[2]We should point out that not all community organizations were antagonistic to the CPD, and not all police activity aroused the anger of community organizations. The CPD's Bureau of Community Services has been active for many years, and its Beat Representative Program has been working with community residents at the grass-roots level since 1977.

[3]They may also get recognized for other reasons-the measures of police work include involvement in community programs (drug programs, schools, senior citizens, etc.); recovered property; development of police-community liaison activities; and other factors as well-but arrests are considered one of the most important measures because they have a direct impact on the offenders.

organizations, and the manipulation of crime statistics. These stories formed a backdrop for explaining every perceived police shortcoming.

On their part, the police felt that member of the public they served, or at least some segments within it, were doing their best to make their jobs more difficult. Not all community organizations were necessarily working for the betterment of their communities; some were working for the betterment of only part of their communities and using crime as a cover for a hidden agenda of restricting racial and ethnic diversity. The police were caught in the middle in these controversies. During a period of major demographic changes in cities, the police also were buffeted by other groups that looked upon them as "pigs," were called fascists by those they were protecting from criminal activity, and were caught between opposing forces in the struggle for civil rights. Consequently, the police often became defensive and cynical about the communities that required the most police protection.

In 1981, against this background of mutual suspicion, the Urban Crime Prevention Program (UCPP) was initiated in Chicago, funded by a federal grant[4] The program focused on reducing crime and the fear of crime in city neighborhoods and improving these neighborhoods by strengthening their community-based organizations. The community-based approach was to be supported by a partnership of citywide resources to support neighborhood crime prevention. Crucial in that partnership were the police and the community.

The grant for the UCPP required the establishment of an advisory council consisting of community groups, police representatives, and other potential members of the partnership. The council was to provide a forum for dialogue and building trust. Given the burden of mutual distrust, it did not take long for things to go wrong. Tensions around questions of community access to police data arose almost immediately. Community organizations had been receiving from the police a 28-day summary report, a tabular report that aggregated all Part I crimes by type for an entire district, with no information about where within the district the incidents occurred. Community organizations participating in the UCPP requested inforrmation that would allow them to see what was happening in their neighborhoods on a block-by-block level. They wanted regular access to the information on the 24-hour activity reports, which were routinely made available to newspapers, university security forces, and some favored community organizations. The CPD, concerned about unauthorized disclosure of confidential information, was reluctant o provide what they considered sensitive information to those organizations that mere often at cross-purposes with them.

---

[4]The UCPP was the forerunner of CANS.

After much negotiation and discussion between the police and community groups, access to information was finally established. Key administrators in the CPD, aware of research that called for changes in policing strategies, became more open to working with community groups. Access was initially in the form of photocopies of the 24-hour activity reports in the relevant districts, but later took the form of monthly computer tapes provided to CANS, listing crime data by district and beat. Each month the tape was picked up at police headquarters and taken to NU, mounted on its mainframe where its format was converted and the data was downloaded to diskettes for use on the Macintosh computers at the CANS office. The data on the tapes included type of crime, time of occurrence, district and beat of occurrence, and block of occurrence, that is, if a crime took place at 5555 West Grand Avenue it was listed as "5500 West Grand Avenue." These data were mapped by CANS and distributed to its member community organizations.

Thus, before the crime mapping project actually started, CANS had been obtaining, mapping, and distributing crime data. Although this access had been routinized and there had been few difficulties associated with the organizations' access to the data, there was still some residual tension between the CPD and CANS prior to the initiation of the planning process leading to the project grant. This led to a very thorough exploration of the nature of the relationship that was to be forged in carrying out the project.

Aside from issues concerning the relationship between the police and community organizations, there was also a residuum of mistrust of university researchers by the CPD. In the late 1960s, as part of the President's Commission on Law Enforcement and Administration of Justice, the CPD (like other major-city police departments) permitted university researchers access in the form of ride-alongs. When these researchers published the results of their research, in which the promised anonymity of police departments was not preserved, the CPD was understandably upset. As a consequence, access by other academics to the CPD for research purposes subsequently became very difficult to obtain. More recently, however, the CPD has opened its doors (and records) to researchers. In 1983, the CPD established a research advisory committee, which a number of researchers from local colleges and universities (including NU and UIC) were invited to join. The department began looking to these individuals for advice on technical and substantive matters, and one of the results of the advisory committee was the crime mapping project.

Regardless of the spirit of cooperation in which the project was conceived, it would seem to be very difficult for the four organizations to work together effectively without major problems. The primary reason, we feel, for our having avoided problems is the fact that, prior to starting the project, we produced a detailed memorandum of understanding, which described the nature of the duties and responsibilities of each of the parties. It was not signed by the research team but rather by officers of the participating organizations. Although we did not cover every eventuality, we apparently addressed enough of them; we never had a major dispute over any of the items covered in the memorandum, the success of which can perhaps be measured by the fact that none of the parties has needed to refer to it. The memorandum of understanding originally agreed to by the four participants is provided in Appendix A. Furthermore, as is described in Chapter 8, agreement has been reached not only at the administrative level but at the working level as well, in substantive areas of common concern: crime, public safety, and policing and patrol strategies.

Relevance to National Institute of Justice Concerns

The relationship between the police and the communities they serve has been a major research focus of the NIJ. For example, the 1988 NIJ Public Safety and Security Program, under which the crime mapping research project was funded, called for research in the following areas:

- Problem-oriented teams that involve the community in identifying particular safety and security concerns and developing new and productive approaches to crime prevention and control.
- Police collaboration with the public and police proactivity in approaching crime.
- Partnership between the police and the private sector to help control nonviolent crime and incivilities.
- Neighborhood actions against crime and fear, by specifically addressing the degree of physical deterioration and social disorder perceived in a neighborhood in terms of their impact on levels of crime and residents' fear.
- Strategies to reverse this process of urban decline and increase the social and economic viability of neighborhoods. For example, examining activities of police, citizens, and business leaders that contribute to controlling or reversing neighborhood deterioration or might assess the effectiveness of coalition strategies designed to target specific neighborhood problems.

This research has focused on these concerns. As will be described in this volume, the crime mapping project has helped to improve relations between the police and the communities they protect, and to have provided information useful to the police in developing new patrol and crime prevention strategies. This information is generated by community residents and businesses, community organizations, and calls for service, both crime- and noncrime-related.

Objectives of the Crime Mapping Project

The overall goal of the crime mapping project was to improve the crime analysis capabilities of the police and community organizations by developing a computerbased mapping system. This goal has been largely accomplished and has been so successful in the 25th District, the pilot district in which it was implemented, that before the project bad completed its first year, a community organization in another district volunteered to purchase computer equipment for that district to enable it to analyze crime in the same manner. In addition, the CPD is currently purchasing mapping systems for the gang crimes unit and the office of the first deputy superintendent along the lines of the system we describe herein, and it is developing functional specifications for a citywide implementation of the Microcomputer-Assisted Police Analysis and Deployment System, (MAPADS). It should also be noted that, even at this pilot level of implementation, the ramifications of this project go beyond Chicago; the population of District 25 is approximately 167,000, the third largest in Chicago and equivalent to that of a medium-size city.

The crime mapping project had five specific objectives that were described in the proposal's work statement:

- To implement the mapping system in its current form for the CPD, including, the provision of maps specifically tailored to police use.
- To analyze the current crime analysis activity in the CPD and in community organizations, paying particular attention to the manner in which a mapping data base management system can assist in analyzing crime data and using the mapping system to see the extent to which it would have assisted in analyzing crime patterns already pursued by the CPD crime analysis unit.
- To evaluate the effectiveness of the computerized mapping system for use by the crime analysis unit, by district personnel, by community organizations, and jointly by these entities.
- To explore the use of calls-for-service (CFS) data (already on computer tape but used primarily for administrative purposes at present by the CPD) within the mapping system, because they may contain a significant amount of information on incivilities and would be relatively easy to include.
- To develop criteria for specific improvements to the mapping system that can be included without redesigning the entire software package, such as the ability to locate an incident on the map automatically, based on its address, and the ability to draw a new map automatically, based on coordinate files provided by the U.S. Census Bureau.

Most of these objectives have been met. Although a formal evaluation (with experimental and control districts) was not originally contemplated–because our primary objective was to implement a mapping system in a patrol district and determine what it could do–we have reached the point at which we feel that such an evaluation is advisable and feasible. During the course of the project we were able to go well beyond its original objectives and study the process of the use of crime incident information for crime prevention and detection purposes in a police department, by community organizations, and jointly by them. Part II of this volume describes the accomplishments of the crime mapping project. To place the accomplishments in their proper perspective, however, it is necessary to understand the technical and administrative context in which the project was initiated. The next three chapters of Part I describe the background and prior research on which the project was built, with respect to crime and incivility data, and the philosophy underlying our technical approach.

CHAPTER 2

Understanding and Using Information About Crime

Implementing a crime mapping system is not a simple task. It involves an understanding of the intricacies of the data that are to be analyzed as well as what kinds of additional data might be usefully analyzed that are not currently used. One needs to understand the nature of the crime data normally collected and analyzed by police, how the data are collected and disseminated, how the police use the data for crime analysis and other purposes, and how community organizations have been involved in crime data analysis.

Crime Data

The police collect crime data for a variety of reasons. Using the data to aid in the apprehension of offenders is a major reason. Offense reports are used by detectives for subsequent follow-up, so the characteristics of each offense are described in detail to help furnish possible clues to the identity of the offender.

Crime statistics are another reason for collecting crime data. Such statistics let community residents know in broad terms what their risk is and how well their police department is doing (Maltz 1977). They serve a legal function as a public record of the events based upon which arrests may be made, and they are used for insurance purposes, so that a victim can make a claim. They also serve administrative functions, providing information to a police department as to how its resources may be allocated more productively.

In one sense these crime data are complete because they describe the circumstances of each event as accurately as the victim and/or witnesses can recall, paying particular attention to any information that would permit the offender to be

20

identified. Yet in another sense they are incomplete because they cannot be easily used to explore crime patterns.[1] For example, the sex, age, identifying features, and clothing worn by an assailant may be described down to the color of his shoelaces. but the geographical and social contexts of the incident-such as the community's perception of dangerousness of the incident's location, what might have brought the victim and/or offender to that location (e.g., open stores, public transit), and other environmental factors (e.g., the type of street lighting; the amount of traffic on the street; the location of bars, parks, abandoned buildings, etc.)-are usually not captured by the incident reporting system because they will ordinarily not contribute to the arrest of the offender. Yet the latter facts affect when and where the crimes are committed and are important in devising crime prevention strategies.

In most instances, police crime data are not designed to facilitate the recognition of such crime patterns, nor are the data presented in a manner designed to be readily comprehensible or useful to officers or others for identifying patterns. These problems of design and presentation are compounded by the incomplete nature of the data, based as they are primarily on the reports of victims. Missing from the police informational data base is the day-to-day social context of crime, which may be understood more completely by community residents than by the police because of the residents' expertise concerning neighborhood problems and activity patterns.

Most people carry a great deal of information in their heads relating to the likelihood of a crime occurring at any given location and time. Police officers, charged with the specific responsibility for doing something about crime, are particularly sensitive as to what constitutes a crime hazard. They implicitly realize the potential impact on crime of school schedules, transit schedules, sporting events, closing times of businesses, darkness, weather, traffic, and other such factors. But because of difficulties in collecting and interpreting such information with existing tools, these community context factors are rarely used in formal crime analysis despite their acknowledged utility.

For community residents, too, there is a wealth of information that affects their perceptions of the safety of their neighborhoods. These perceptions are formed not only by crime data. Graffiti, rowdiness, public drunkenness, abandoned autos, and other such factors may be as influential in coloring perceptions and appear as threatening as victim-oriented crime. These factors. called incivilities in the research literature, are discussed more fully in Chapter 3.

For the most part, however, the data used to analyze crime patterns by the police and others are generated by the police in their response to citizens' calls for service. The next section describes the way the CPD handles data relating to these calls for service. It is similar to the way most other large police departments perform the same functions.

Data Handling in the Chicago Police Department

[1] The CPD uses the term *pattern* in a specific way; see the section headed Police Crime Pattern Analysis. In the current section we use the term in its more general meaning.

When a call comes in on the 911 emergency lines, the call taker fills out a radio dispatch card. If appropriate, the call taker may suggest that the caller request service from another municipal agency or may refer the incident to the CPD's Call-Back Unit, which can take a case report over the telephone. If the incident requires a responding officer, the dispatcher selects a patrol officer to respond to the call. The first choice for response is, of course, the officer patrolling the beat from which the call originated, but in the event that the beat officer is on another call or is otherwise out of service, another patrol officer is dispatched. Information on the radio dispatch card is then read over the air to that patrol officer. The card is subsequently sent to the Data Systems Division so that it can be keyed into the mainframe computer for storage on a data tape. Fig. 2.1 shows some of the primary routes taken by dispatch and offense information.

In those cases for which a case report is required, a unique Records Division number is assigned for linking follow-up reports to the original dispatch. The following information from the case reports is also keyed into the computer: type of offense, victim and offender data, dates, time, location code. and other identifiers. However, the narrative is not among the data fields keyed in.[2] The case report information is not only stored on a data tape, but is also stored on the computer's disk drives for instant access.

Dispatch data are rarely used for tactical or resource allocation purposes after entry into the computer. Although a report summarizing the daily dispatch activity of each district is prepared and distributed to the district within a week and is used for administrative and supervisory purposes, the sheer volume of incidents precludes their use for tactical purposes except in special cases. More recently, however. the CFS data have been analyzed for repeat offenders, and this information has been provided to district commanders to permit them to consider different response strategies for locations that generate a great deal of repeat calls.

Offense report data, on the other hand, are entered into the Case Report Information and Management Evaluation (CRIMES) data base, which is accessible using the RAMIS data base management system, the system used by the CPD on its mainframe computer. Access to the data base is limited, however, because extensive searches of CRIMES would tie up the mainframe for too long a time. In addition, because relatively few detectives are familiar with RAMIS and because the case narrative is not included in the data base. the utility of the CRIMES data base in searching for patterns is limited. Of particular note is the fact that the case report

narrative is not on the data base. Virtually all detectives state that in order to get a feel for the case, they need to read the case narrative.

Most incidents do not require case reports; for example, if a disturbance is handled

[2]This is currently true for most police departments, but should change as departments move to providing handheld computers for patrol officers for their report preparation. The CPD plans to implement such an innovation as part of its new computer-aided dispatch system, which is currently being designed.

on the spot and requires no additional follow-up, the officer reports back to the dispatcher, using a miscellaneous coding system (Fig. 2.2). The dispatcher then writes the code on the dispatch card. If an incident does require a follow-up report, the appropriate code is written on the dispatch card. In either case the dispatcher puts the cards in a pile that is sent to the data entry clerks for later keying into the computer. Because these cards have a low priority for entry (compared to the entry of case reports), depending on the volume of activity there may be a delay of a few days before the CFS data are entered into the computer.

Case reports are prepared by the patrol officers in duplicate. The originals are sent to police headquarters, where before they are keyed into the computer four copies are made of each and sent to the appropriate investigative units. Then the original is sent to the Records Division for entry into the computer. One reason for the preparation of so many copies is that detectives from different units need to read the narrative.[3] In addition, depending on the case volume and day of the week, it can take a few days for these case reports to be entered. Therefore, paper is the medium whereby information flows in the CPD, and the flow appears to be both endless and irreplaceable. As one detective put it, "If the Xerox machine is down, we might just as well close up shop and all go home." However, this should change with the implementation of the CPD's Office Automation Services and Information System (OASIS), which is currently being developed.

A carbon copy of the case report is retained by the district. Before it is filed, it is checked by the review officer, whose job it is to ensure that case reports are filled out properly. The review officer also uses the case reports to prepare a 24-hour activity report for the district commander, describing the felony (and serious misdemeanor) activity in the district for the past 24 hours. A district commander needs to keep abreast of the district's crime activity on a daily basis; the 24-hour activity report (see again Fig. 2.1) is the vehicle that makes this possible. The watch commander's log, which describes serious and unusual incidents, provides the district commander with additional information on what happened on the previous day. Prepared before 9:00 a.m. every morning, the 24-hour activity report permits commanders to determine what is happening in their districts long before the computer data become available. This report was necessitated by the delays of up to 3 days in obtaining offense data

---

[3]The Los Angeles Police Department makes even more copies of its case reports (LAPD 1988). If, for example, an elderly Asian woman is assaulted by a Hispanic gang member, additional copies will be sent to the Asian crime unit, the racial incident unit, the gang crimes unit, and the unit dealing with crimes against the elderly. If the incident is expected to make the news, copies of the case report must be sent to the top administrators and the public information office as well.

from CPD headquarters. This had been a problem before the CPD computerized its incident reports and has not been alleviated by computerization.

The 24-hour activity report has been in use in the CPD for almost 20 years. However, it is not a totally complete record of activity in the district because of the following three factors:

- No information is given about certain police-generated activity such as arrests for prostitution or narcotics offenses.
- Some calls to 911 are routed to call-back officers, who take the information over the phone and fill out a case report. This differential response policy was adopted by the CPD to limit dispatching patrol officers to only those calls that require an officer present. The call-back officer's case report will also be sent to the district after a short delay and will appear on a later 24-hour activity report.
- Victims sometimes go to a district other than the district of occurrence to report a crime. For example, a person whose car was vandalized near his house overnight may report it at the downtown station during his lunch hour. This case report will be filled out with the proper beat of occurrence and sent to the proper district, where it will show up on a later 24-hour activity report.

In the latter two cases, the data will be delayed for a day or two before it gets to the district.

Despite the limitations of crime data as currently collected, they are used by the police in a variety of ways. The next section describes some of these uses.

Police Crime Pattern Analysis

Analysis of patterns of crime and noncrime calls for service has been used extensively by police departments for allocating manpower across shifts and patrol cars across beats. These developments, funded by NIJ and other agencies, resulted in the Hypercube model (Larson, 1975) and patrol car allocation model (PCAM), (Chaiken & Dormont, 1978), and others. These models, however, focus on departmental administrative and resource allocation matters-such as drawing beat boundaries for equalizing workloads-rather than on offense patterns for investigating, preventing, or deterring crimes. Both manual and computer-based techniques have been used for this latter activity.

Graphical crime pattern analysis in the form of *pin maps* has been used in police departments for many years. Typically, an analyst puts a pin representing a crime on a map to note how the crime clusters around other crimes (distinguished, perhaps, by different colored pins), the land use characteristics of the location (i.e., near a park or school), and so on. The mechanical task of plotting the crimes is independent of any other data management or analytic task and must be kept up-to-date to be of any use. As the characteristics of the crime or the location multiply, or as the crimes proliferate, the density and complexity of the map can become unmanageable. Severely limited choices have to be made about which dimensions of data to display with different pins, or the data have to be culled frequently. However, culling undated or indistinguishable pins can be a burdensome task. The analyst must either remember other characteristics of crimes or search manually through a separate file to tie locations to crimes. Under these circumstances, the maps frequently fall into disuse.

Computer analysis of crime patterns for investigative purposes began in the early 1970s in the Us Angeles Police Department, through the use of a system called Pattern Recognition for Investigating Crime (PATRIC). Since that time other computer-based techniques have been proposed and used. For example, in one department a data base was developed and used to determine which arrestees lived in the neighborhood where a crime occurred (Savage, 1978). More recently, a system has been used to search for crime patterns based on an offense data base (McGehee & Whiteacre, 1983; "Police and Computer," 1981; Robertson & Chang, 1980). These systems are based primarily on sophisticated computer algorithms that look for patterns within the collected data.

An automatic means of depicting crime graphically was developed by the St. Louis Police Department, using an IBM mainframe computer (Carnaghi & McEwen, 1970; Pauly, McEwen, & Finch, 1967). The St. Louis police used SYMAP, a line printer mapping program. Based on this pioneering effort, this use of computers spread to police departments throughout the United States. Although a computer-aided approach to crime analysis was promoted as a means of using computers to fight crime, the actual results fell far short of the promises made. The patterns they found were by and large well-known, for example, that crimes occur more frequently on weekend evenings and in low-income areas, and that most victims are low-income minorities.

With the advent of commercially available graphics software that interacts with data base management systems, a number of police departments have begun to display their incident information on video screens driven by computers (Williams, 1986). Although the police use the maps primarily for resource allocation purposes, the displays have also been useful for investigative purposes as automated pin maps.

In a current project at Northeastern University's Center for Applied Social Research, researchers have been working with the Boston Police Department to map its crime data. For the most part, the mapping has been done by hand; the aim has been to develop a system that would use graphics-oriented work stations (e.g., Sun or Apollo) to do the graphics automatically. One of the findings of this project is that there were significant discrepancies between the category of event as defined by the victim/witness and by the responding officer. The project also includes some examples of how patterns of criminal activity shifted over time in certain Boston neighborhoods.[4]

Another crime analysis project using computer graphics is under way at the Illinois Criminal Justice Information Authority (ICJIA). Under a grant from the U.S. Bureau of Justice Statistics, ICJIA's study is called the Spatial and Temporal Analysis of Crime (STAC). The ICJIA project is focused on the use of maps to locate concentrations of criminal activity in Chicago suburbs, using cluster analysis algorithms. It is based on ICJIA's Police Information Management System (PIMS), a centralized system that serves a number of suburbs in greater Chicago. This system maintains the crime data for the subscribing departments and permits them to manipulate the data for their own and other (e.g., UCR) uses. The STAC system is an add-on that permits the department to map the crimes within their jurisdictional boundaries.

Another computer-based project of interest took place in St. Petersburg, Florida. he St. Petersburg Police Department conducted an NIJ-sponsored project entitled paperless Information System-Totally On-Line (PISTOL). Although this project not specifically a crime mapping project, its characteristics lend themselves to the incorporation of mapping. Incident reports are not handwritten but are typed into handheld computers. Although the computer reports are then converted into paper reports, the capability exists for them to be entered directly into the department's mainframe computer. Similarly, such information could be entered and mapped onto a district's computer or terminal for immediate presentation to the commander and others of district- and beat-wide activity.

Thus, computers have begun to prove themselves to be more and more useful in the acquisition, display, and analysis of crime data. However, as Goldstein (1979) points out, the limitations of crime analysis have to do with not only with the data and but with the fact that "these analyses are almost always put to very limited use-to apprehend a professional car thief or a well-known cat burglar-rather than rethinking, the overall police response to the problem of car theft and cat burglaries."

Crime Analysis in the Chicago Police Department

In order to better understand some of the problems with past computer-based analytic methods, a description of the common practice in noncomputerized crime pattern analysis would be instructive. In this section we describe the way crime analysis is carried out in the CPD's crime analysis unit (CAU); it is similar to crime analysis units in other urban police departments.

The CAU is a centralized unit within the detective division. In addition, analysis

[4]A meeting sponsored by the Illinois Criminal Justice Information Authority (ICJIA) was held on September 9, 1987, to enable those working in the crime mapping field to share information. Presentations were given by Glenn Pierce of Northeastern University, Boston, and by several representatives of the crime mapping project and of the ICJIA.

tasks are performed in areas and some districts (although analysis is not a formal assignment in district). The standard procedure in the CAU is for detectives to specialize in a particular offense type (e.g., robbery, sexual assault, auto theft) and to read all the reports of that type that come in from throughout the city. These analysts rely on their memory and on paper filing systems, organized by beat of occurrence and/or by their own individualized modus operandi (MO) classification systems. Even with a set of standard classification criteria, analysts rely primarily on their memory (as informed by their own prior experience) to identify crime patterns. That is, different analysts use different classification systems based on their own perceptions of what constitutes a pattern, their own experience, and their own memory to identify crime patterns. They are of the opinion that a single classification system, computerized or not, is not likely to be of use to them. One of the consequences of this is that continuity is lost when a member of the CAU retires or is given a new assignment.

The CPD distinguishes two types of patterns: (a) those that point to the characteristics of a particular perpetrator(s), (e.g., physical appearance, dress, behaviors repeated in committing crimes), and (b) those that identify a type of crime and a geographical pattern when little information is known about the offenders. The former are reported internally in crime analysis patterns and the latter in information bulletins (see Appendix C). Formally, a crime analysis pattern is the association of two or more particular criminal activities with an individual or group of individuals believed responsible for the crimes, whereas an information bulletin is issued in recognition of the same situation when insufficient information is available to determine if the same offender or group of offenders is responsible for the commission of the crimes. The CAU's aim in these activities is to assist the field units in apprehending offenders (i.e., to clear crime patterns). As a detective division unit, analysts are understandably more interested in the use of crime pattern analysis for apprehension purposes than they are in identifying geographic patterns that might be useful for crime prevention. Of course, apprehending offenders leads to crime prevention in that the offenders are no longer available to commit crimes. However, by crime prevention we mean proactive efforts other than apprehension to deter offenders. The general information bulletins, also produces by the CAU, can be considered preventive in nature.

Prior to this project, the CAU had made limited use of crime maps. It previously had used citywide pin maps, but they were discontinued in 1979. They were hard to use, always seemed to show approximately the same geographic distribution of crime, and were not very helpful in identifying the perpetrators of specific crimes.

The CAU has made some use of computers for developing crime patterns. As mentioned earlier, the CPD uses RAMIS, a database management system, to analyze the data it stores on CRIMES, a computerized data base of crime reports. However, RAMIS and CRIMES can only be used as a first cut for generating patterns; as previously mentioned, CRIMES does not include the narrative portion of the case reports and thus is of limited use in analyzing MO-based patterns. The CAU analysts do not believe that a standardized set of MO categories in a computerized data base would be as useful as their memories and the idiosyncratic connections they make based on their daily reading and hand filing of every case report; that is, the analysts have distinct ways of searching for patterns based on their individual experience.[5] It appears that CRIMES is used primarily to answer questions put to the CAU by others outside the unit, for example, as to the number of crimes of a certain type that have occurred in a given district over a specified time period. Analysts cannot answer questions of this type by using their hand filing system, because they regularly remove from the files cases over 1 month old (except for sexual assault and homicide cases). In fact, detectives rarely use the computer for exploratory analyses of crime data. Searches on the mainframe take a long time, especially if the search covers a long time period. The fact that the mainframe is in almost constant use for administrative purposes and routine crime analyses makes it difficult for detectives to do exploratory analyses.

From this description, we note the following:

- Each CAU analyst appears to have his or her own method of analyzing case reports.
- A computerized system that cannot be easily mastered will probably not be accepted.
- A computerized MO system that cannot be individualized will probably not be accepted.
- Maps that take more manpower to maintain than the potential insight they provide will not be used.
- Reading through (and hand filing) every case report gives the analysts a feel for the case.

From our discussions with police analysts in other departments, it appears that this description is typical, and this is apparently why computerized crime analysis systems have been put to limited use. Specific pattern-searching algorithms generated by a systems analyst may be too general to be of much use, and even algorithms based on the procedures of a good detective are probably unique to that detective and not generalizable to other detectives. However, there have been many changes in the way data base management systems are conceived, that make them more user-friendly and able to accommodate individual idiosyncracies.

The reason for the lack of complete reliance on CRIMES and RAMIS has much to do with the characteristics of data base management systems that are available on mainframe computer systems. A data base management system (DBMS) permits a user

---

[5]We performed a preliminary experiment to determine whether an abridged version of a case narrative entered in a data base by Detective A would be entered in essentially the same manner by Detective B. so that all would "see" the same incident when reading the computer file. Although there were some difficulties in performing the experiment, it appeared that with some standardization of nomenclature a useful data base incorporating narratives could be implemented.

to manipulate files of data. In the case of the crime mapping project, the files are the file of crime reports and the file of incivilities, if available. The user should be able to enter. edit, and delete file records, and should be able to search for and select records with specific characteristics (e.g.. time of occurrence. type of crime). These records can then be used for further processing; for example, if the file is of financial data, one might perform arithmetic operations on them. The further processing in our case may also be graphical; some DBMSs have the ability to select records with specific characteristics and depict their occurrence on a computer-generated map.

The DBMS packages most familiar to social scientists are those used for data analysis, in particular Statistical Package for the Social Sciences (SPSS) or Statistical Analysis System (SAS); RAMIS, used by the CPD, is another popular mainframe DBMS. These are relatively difficult to learn and use, but from the standpoint of the users they have been worthwhile learning because they permit the user to do the following:

1. store data records in data files;
2. edit data records as necessary;
3. prepare tables and reports;
4. choose a specific subset of data records (e.g., all robberies that occur between 3:00 p.m. and 5:00 p.m.) on which to conduct an analysis; and
5. analyze the data using various statistical techniques included in the software packages.

All of these characteristics can be found in the new generation of DBMS software available for personal computers, with one difference: The newer packages are considerably easier to learn and use than the mainframe DBMSs. Furthermore, they go well beyond the characteristics mentioned above in terms of what they permit users to do. Also, SPSS, SAS, and RAMIS now have DBMS software for personal computers; these versions are much more user-friendly than their mainframe counterparts.

An important reason for ease of learning and use is that the market for this kind of software has grown tremendously. Whereas the market for mainframe-based software was restricted to the relatively small number of mainframe computers, perhaps numbering in the thousands. the market for the new generations of microcomputer-based DBMS software numbers in the millions. It is for this reason that the competition for the most useful and user-friendly DBMS has resulted in relatively inexpensive software packages that can be learned in an afternoon and used immediately, even by people relatively unsophisticated in computers.

One of the most important attributes of a DBMS for crime analysis is that it provides the ability to search through an entire data base to select specific records that have certain attributes (e.g., all rapes occurring in the 4th district that took place within an hour of sunset when it was raining or snowing, in which a knife was used and the offender wore a ski mask and warned the victim not to move for 10 minutes). What makes this task difficult from the standpoint of the police is that not all of these data elements are indexed-weather may be a coded field on the case report; time till dusk can be calculated from the *time* field; and type of weapon is coded, but the peculiarities of the offenders are not. New types of DBMSs are now available that have the ability to index and search for key words in the text portion of case reports, so that words such as mask and warned could be included in the search. Furthermore, search techniques have improved to the point where thousands of records can be searched in only a few minutes. This throughput is actually faster than that achievable by mainframe computers because the user does not have to wait until his or her job is called up on a queue. Moreover, the user can see the results on a screen and have them printed out immediately.

A number of DBMSs tied to graphics packages have been developed, primarily for personal computers (although some have recently been developed for mainframes as well). Their advantages for crime analysis would be self-evident if, after displaying all of the above-mentioned rapes on a map, the analyst were to notice that they were all within one block of a subway entrance. In fact, a situation in which a map would have been helpful did occur, according to one of the detectives who worked on the crime mapping project. A man had been going to schoolyards throughout the north side of the city and exposing himself to young children. After he was caught it was discovered that he lived close to downtown, worked in a northern suburb, and commuted on one of the city's diagonal avenues (Lincoln Avenue). Had the incidents been mapped, it would have shown that the schools were all within a block or two of Lincoln Avenue.

Cooperative Crime Analysis

Crime analysis is not the exclusive province of police departments nor of specialized units within departments. Community organizations may also become involved in this activity. Cooperative crime analysis refers to analysis of crime data that is not exclusively within police departments. It may mean that other organizations use the police data or that the police interact with other organizations as part of their analysis work. In either instance it represents efforts by the police and community organizations to tap each other's resources in investigating crime and its impact on the community. The experience in Chicago is described prior to the start of the crime mapping project; also described are efforts in other communities.

The Chicago Experience

The CPD interacts with community organizations in a number of ways, based on their common interest in neighborhood anticrime efforts. The Beat Representative Program is one means by which the police and the community cooperate on matters related to crime. Begun in 1977, it has grown to include almost 18,000 volunteers who deal with the CPD through its salaried citizen employees. In addition, for many years there have been numerous block watches organized by community-based organizations to enhance neighborhood safety.

CANS has organized volunteer neighborhood anticrime efforts, working to spread block watch and other crime prevention programs (e.g., school watch and business watch) throughout the city. It provides training and technical assistance to community-based organizations. In addition, using the data provided by the CPD, CANS has been distributing crime maps to community organizations since 1985. The maps are discussed, patterns are searched for, organizing targets are selected, rumors are squelched, and educational priorities are determined by the community organizations.

The South Shore Commission, a community organization affiliated with CANS, was an early user of computer maps of crimes and incivilities in its crime prevention program. The maps have been used extensively in determining where block meetings should be held and in educating people at the meetings about the extent and nature of their particular problems. As evidence of the need for action, the maps have also been used successfully by block watch participants in meetings with neighborhood landlords. In one neighborhood, problem buildings and hot spots[6] were added to the incident maps. I Residents then took the maps to the landlords of the buildings and used them to reinforce their case that lack of landlord investment and tenant screening were seriously contributing to neighborhood problems. Commitments were received for a spring fix-up and better tenant screening from several of the building owners.

Aside from these purely volunteer efforts, the city of Chicago has taken steps as well. Before the crime mapping project began, the Chicago Intervention Network (CIN) was created in response to increasing gang violence and the evident willingness of people to get involved in doing something concrete about it. In addition to a staff of street workers, CIN funds 30 community organizations that are engaged in block watch organizing, school patrols and other crime prevention strategies.

Experiences in Other Jurisdictions

Efforts to achieve satisfactory levels of citizen cooperation are under way in many communities. Some of these cooperative efforts, as in Chicago, involve community meetings and redeployment of police efforts in response to community initiatives. Increasing numbers of police departments have been exploring other ways to disseminate useful information to citizens. Houston, for example, has been using police to tell citizens about crime patterns and effective ways to protect themselves; in addition, its Neighborhood-Oriented Policing effort, implemented in the area served by its West Side Command Station, recognizes that patrol officers can (and should) be involved in problem solving, planning, and community organizing (Dodenhoff. 1989). In some communities (e.g.. Mt. Prospect, Illinois, and Oxnard, California) cable television is used to relay information about crime. In Ann Arbor, Michigan, color-coded maps depicting criminal incidents are included in a weekly newspaper; the Fenway community of Boston uses maps similarly. And in Evanston,

---

[6]A hot spot has a fairly definite meaning to community organizations and residents. This concept is discussed fully in Chapter 3.

Illinois, targeted mailings are sent to each household, locating recent crimes by type on neighborhood-specific lists and conveying information about ways to respond to the crime problem.

A crime analysis project in Newport News, Virginia, funded by NIJ, looked at the social context of crime more than had been done previously (Eck & Spelman, 1985). Based on Goldstein's (1979) ideas about problem-oriented policing, the Newport News project used resources beyond the police department in addressing problems that appeared at first look to be purely police problems. In one case a pattern of burglaries in an apartment complex was resolved by turning to housing agencies for help. In another, a pattern of intrafamily homicides prompted a homicide detective to develop contacts with social service agencies as well as prosecutors and judges so that individuals responsible for generating multiple domestic disturbance cases were given the option of going into counseling or to jail.

One major difference between the cooperative crime analysis as practiced in Chicago and in most other jurisdictions is that, in other cities, police-community cooperation usually means that the *community* provides the *police* with information. Although this is also true in Chicago, community organizations in Chicago have a formal mechanism for *receiving* data from the CPD. Atlanta, too, in its Partnership Against Crime program, is committed to generating citizen participation in planning and crime-fighting efforts, and to the joint identification and prioritizing of crime problems.

In Chicago, however, the emphasis has been on providing crime data to community organizations in a form suitable for analysis. Prior to the start of the crime mapping project, CANS began receiving from the CPD a monthly computer tape of criminal incidents. This transfer of data has continued up to the present. In addition, as part of the project, CANS began receiving from the CPD, and distributing to some of its member organizations in District 25, a map-based data base, which further enhanced CANS's crime analysis capabilities. In addition to its work in District 25, CANS has used its expertise to develop map-based data bases for other member organizations not in the 25th District, using, the monthly crime data tapes provided CANS by the CPD. In particular, it is now easier for CANS to combine police crime data with its own information on hazards and incivilities.

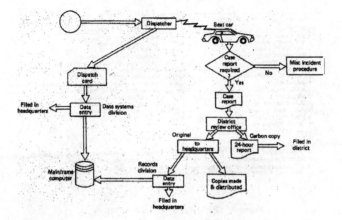

Figure 2.1. CPD dispatch and
case report flow chart.

MISCELLANEOUS INCIDENT REPORTING TABLE			Use the following table to report all miscellaneous incidents. Select the correct incident and police action from the table and state correct number and phonetic letter or letters to the dispatcher when you return to service.
CPD-11.484 (Rev. 7/83)		CHICAGO POLICE	
1. DISTURBANCE, DOMESTIC		A - ADAM	NOT BONA FIDE INCIDENT
2. DISTURBANCE, TEENAGERS		B - BOY	NO PERSON CAN BE FOUND
3. DISTURBANCE, DRUNK		C - CHARLES	NO SUCH ADDRESS
4. DISTURBANCE, NOISE		D - DAVID	NO POLICE SERVICE NECESSARY
5. DISTURBANCE, OTHER		E - EDWARD	PERPETRATOR GONE ON POLICE ARRIVAL
6. ILLEGAL PARKING		F - FRANK	PEACE RESTORED
7. SICK REMOVAL/CONFINEMENT		G - GEORGE	ADVISED WARRANT
8. INJURED PERSON	POLICE ACTION	H - HENRY	ADVISED TO RECONTACT POLICE IF REPEATED/RETURNED
9. MAN OR WOMAN DOWN		*I - IDA	REMOVED TO HOSPITAL OR DETOXIFICATION FACILITY
**10. ANIMAL BITE		J - JOHN	RETURNED TO FAMILY OR HOME
11. SUSPICIOUS PERSON(S)/AUTO		K - KING	TAKEN TO DISTRICT STATION
12. CITIZEN CALLING FOR HELP		L - LINCOLN	INFORMATION REPORT SUBMITTED
13. LOST PERSON FOUND		M - MARY	ISSUED TRAFFIC CITATION
14. AUTO, BURGLAR OR HOLDUP ALARM		N - NORA	ISSUED ORDINANCE COMPLAINT
15. INHALATOR		O - OCEAN	ADVISED LEGAL HELP
16. FIRE		P - PAUL	OTHER POLICE SERVICE
17. ESCORT		R - ROBERT	ARREST MADE
18. TRAFFIC ACCIDENT		X - X-RAY	MISCELLANEOUS INCIDENT EXCEPTION REPORT COMPLETED
19. OTHER MISCELLANEOUS INCIDENT		Y - YOUNG	ANIMAL BITE INFORMATION REPORT

* MISCELLANEOUS INCIDENT EXCEPTION REPORT REQUIRED IN EVERY BONA FIDE CASE.
** ANIMAL BITE INFORMATION REPORT REQUIRED IN EVERY BONA FIDE CASE.

Figure 2.2. The coding system used to report
incidents that require no follow-up.

CHAPTER 3

Understanding and Using
Information About Incivilities

Information about specific crimes is not the only safety-related information available
to (or useful to) the police or the community. Safety is a multifaceted issue, and crime
is only one aspect (an important one, to be sure). This chapter focuses on the nature
of incivilities, which are acts or situations that may not be criminal, but that have an
adverse effect on a community. The extent to which police data can be used to
provide information about incivilities, and thus improve community safety, is
described as well. Also discussed are the nature of the community's perceptions of
dangerous locations, or hot spots.

Incivilities

Cities have reputations for being relatively safe or unsafe. So do neighborhoods, and
so do specific locales within neighborhoods. Although it is well-known that these
reputations are poorly correlated with crime rates (Skogan & Maxfield, 1981), only
recently have we begun to understand the dynamics that underlie an area's reputation.
A number of scholars have begun to clarify the dimensions that have an impact on
perceptions of neighborhood safety. Biderman, Johnson, McIntyre, and Weir (1967)
were among the earliest observers to speculate that routine boisterousness,
drunkenness, and other incivilities–experienced far more frequently than crime
victimization-may be as influential in coloring perceptions of crime and may be as
threatening as victim-oriented crime.

Although the collection or analysis of such data is not currently among the
priorities of police departments, a wealth of studies since 1967 (e.g., Garofalo, 1977;
Dubow, McCabe, and Kaplan, 1979; Lavrakas et al., 1981) has provided a rich body
of evidence that these behaviors are important to citizens in how they characterize the
safety of their environment. In various studies, for example, public behavior such as
pushing and vulgarity is seen as more annoying than what the police define as a crime
(American Transit Association, 1973); environmental problems such as trash and
noise are cited more frequently as neighborhood problems than are crimes

(Metropolitan Washington Council of Governments, 1974); and traditionally defined crime and the fear of crime are found to be lower in neighborhoods where reported incivilities, such as teenagers hanging out, are lower (Skogan & Maxfield, 1981).

In 1978, Hunter conceptualized the relationship between social disorders, crime, incivility, and fear of victimization in some detail, tracing the roots of the concept through various strains of social science literature (e.g., Becker, 1967; Geertz, 1963; Shils, 1975). Hunter proposed that "incivility has a greater impact on fear than does crime itself." More recently, social scientists have begun to explore and detail the complexity of the interrelationships among relevant variables (see, for example, the work of Taylor and his colleagues, discussed below).

The use of the term *incivilities* in this volume is merely an attempt to capture and acknowledge the fact that community definitions of fear-generating activity can depart markedly from definitions based on police statistics. In a major work in this domain, Merry (1981) has noted that

dangerous experiences include far more than crime. Insults, mockery, racial slurs, harassment, and flirtatious sexual comments that assault a person's sense of order, propriety, and self-respect awaken feelings of danger even when they contain no threat of actual physical violence. The deterioration of the moral order of a neighborhood, including bad influences of street youths, the prevalence of drunks, neglectful parents, and people who live according to different moral codes, evoke feelings that the neighborhood is dangerous... Danger is evident in the downhill slide in a neighborhood: trash, broken fences, graffiti, rusting cars, and general appearance of neglect suggest that no one cares about the neighborhood. (p. 143)

Merry concludes that "such subtle signals may contribute to the inexplicable 'loss of faith' in urban neighborhoods that often puzzles planners and politicians" (p. 144). Taylor, Shumaker, and Gottfredson (1985), in a detailed analysis from Baltimore, show how this, too, may be conditional. They find, for example, that the impact of physical parameters (e.g., housing layout, traffic volume, and litter) is especially crucial in shaping residents' perceptions of their locales in moderate-income neighborhoods "where SES (socio-economic status) is neither so high as to guarantee confidence, nor so low as to guarantee pessimism" (p. 274).

The fear of crime itself may have an impact on neighborhood cohesion, instilling distrust and suspicion among fellow residents. Thus, people may become afraid to venture into unsafe areas or even to leave their homes. In Wilson's (1975) telling phrase, crime may atomize society and "make of its individual members mere calculators estimating their own advantage" (p. 21). People are less likely to intervene to help one another, and the crime rate may climb.

The relationship between neighborhood-generated and police-generated definitions of crime-related activity appears to be extremely complex. The differing conceptions held by community residents and the police have a significant effect on what is thought of as criminal or crime-relevant, on what is reported to the police, and on how neighborhoods and locales come to have varying reputations.

Crimes that are central enough to police to be treated as index crimes are not necessarily as central to the concerns of community residents, whereas incidents that appear less important to police may be crucial to community residents in defining the safety of their neighborhoods. For example, Merry (1981) argues that even though larcenies–thefts without personal confrontation–are classified as serious by police, they were far less serious to the citizens she studied. If larcenies are reported to the police, it is in the hopes of recovering lost goods or for insurance purposes rather than because of their impact on one's sense of safety. In contrast, acts of violence committed by strangers are thought of as serious, regardless of whether a formal crime is committed or whether much property is stolen. And residents may regard assaults as crimes only if they are by strangers; assaults by friends or acquaintances may not be reported to the police or on victimization surveys (Kalish, 1974; Turner, 1972).

Moreover, although police business may be relatively well-defined from the perspective of the police, boundaries between bureaucratic entities (e.g., between departments of police, housing. and sanitation) are less clear or relevant to citizens. Thus, incidents that seem less important to police (or that fall outside of their mandate) may be crucial to residents in defining the safety of their neighborhoods.

In her imaginative use of resident-produced maps of neighborhoods, Merry (1981) compared their nominations of dangerous areas with the distribution of robberies from a victimization survey. Areas of a neighborhood can be considered safe by police but unsafe by some community residents. Cognitive maps of safety may nominate different areas of a community, for entirely different reasons. Safe locales are not necessarily crime-free, nor are dangerous locales those where crime is most frequent. Signals of danger include narrow, enclosed pathways, even where crimes rarely occur. Merry describes danger as

a cognitive assessment of cues that lead an individual to anticipate fear in a situation. These cues are structured into spatial, temporal and personal cognitive maps that define the places, times and categories of persons who are likely to be safe or dangerous. The decision that a situation is or is not dangerous depends on the intersection of these maps. To understand the fear of crime. it is less useful to ask how afraid an individual feels than it is to explore the content of his or her cognitive maps (p. 11).

Familiarity is a crucial variable; known locales are generally perceived as safer (e.g., one's own side of a housing project, be it the periphery to those living in the center, or the center to those living on the edge). The area in front of one's own house seems safe whereas police crime statistics indicate that two thirds of all robberies occur there. People who know street youths are significantly more likely to find housing projects less dangerous, regardless of their victimization experience (Merry, 1981; see also Gould & White, 1974 and Springer, 1974).

Neighborhoods can be more or less successful in contributing to their own safety. Kelling and Stewart (1989) list the different factors that may help defend a neighborhood against crime and disorder, both individually and collectively, by banding together informally or into formal organizations. both in conjunction with private or public police. Individuals who attempt to protect themselves from neighborhood efforts to the exclusion of any collective action may detract from rather than contribute to community safety.

Variables also interact with one another in complex ways. For example, perceptions of the danger of crime in areas of a neighborhood differ among ethnic groups (not predictable from rates of victimization), and danger is differentially inspired by strangers (Merry, 1981; see also Taylor, Gottfredson & Brower, 1985, for related findings on the relationship between racial diversity and neighborhood attachment). In summary, incivility refers to several interrelated phenomena. In every case it describes neighborhood conditions that people perceive to indicate a dangerous or threatening situation. The conditions themselves may or may not have a connection with crime, or even with danger as seen by others, but the point here is that some portion of a community's residents make that connection.

Within the broad concept of incivilities we distinguish physical *conditions*-such as boarded up buildings, vacant lots, littered alleys, or gang graffiti-from social *behaviors*-such as groups of youths making public remarks that others may interpret as threatening. The physical conditions may convey a pervasive sense of social deterioration, whereas the social behaviors often impose a more immediate sense of social discomfort. Frequently, the uncivil quality of social behaviors may be traced to cultural differences between those who are carrying on the behavior and those who are made to feel uncomfortable or threatened. These cultural differences can often be derived from ethnic differences, generational differences, or the combination of the two (e.g., elderly Poles sharing the urban streets with young Latinos).

Many (but not all) of these incivilities provoke a call for police service. Although the police do not ordinarily fill out reports on such incidents, they do collect a limited amount of information about them. The data may be used to develop administrative statistics (e.g., on how long different types of calls take to service) or they will be consulted along with the taped telephone call and radio dispatch communications when it becomes necessary to trace a particular incident from start to finish. However, these incidents are not a high priority for data collection. Police departments are generally UCR-driven, that is, they respond to the increase in the Crime Index as measured by the FBI's UCRs, which are more than enough to handle, but do not concern themselves overly with the less serious incidents grouped under the rubric incivilities.[1]

Furthermore, police departments are charged with the collection of an enormous amount of information related to crime. This takes a great deal of time; a felony report may take anywhere from 15 minutes to 2 hours to complete, depending on the type of

---

[1]In the 1930s, the FBI began to publish the *Index of Crime*, which is based on the voluntary reporting of crime statistics by police departments to the FBI. At first, the *Index of Crime* consisted of seven crimes-murder, rape, robbery, aggravated assault, burglary, larceny ($50 and over), and auto theft-that were included in Part I of the form that was sent to the FBI; other crimes were included in Part 11 of that form. Thus, the crimes that form the *Index of Crime* have also been called Part I offenses. Subsequently, the larceny category was broadened to include all larcenies, and arson was added to the *Index of Crime*. See Maltz (1977) for a discussion of these issues.

crime, the availability of witnesses, the competence of the officer in obtaining information and evidence, the amount of other activity in the police district at the time, and other factors. If a requirement were added that reports were to be written for all incivilities as well, the effectiveness of the police department might be severely compromised. In fact, the trend is in the opposite direction-toward reducing the reporting workload of the police. Even in the late 1960s, the Chicago and Boston police departments decided to reduce their reporting requirements by permitting officers to call into their dispatchers with a code indicating the disposition of incidents for which a case report was not required (Maltz & Waldron, 1968–see again Figure 2.2). In a more recent example of reducing the reporting workload of the police, the St. Petersburg Police Department gave its patrol officers portable computers. According to Sergeant Maurice McGough, the St. Petersburg police estimate that the computers have reduced their report-writing time by 40%. Other departments have instituted the policy of having specific teams of officers take reports of offenses that do not require immediate response or of requiring the victims of certain crimes to go to the station house to make their reports. Therefore, we cannot expect police officers to begin writing up offense reports for incivilities regardless of their utility, at least in the near term.

Thus, we are confronted with a dilemma with important philosophical and practical consequences: The data most obviously useful to the police may not be the most salient to neighborhood residents in their efforts to make their communities safer and less vulnerable to crime. Crime data, when collected and analyzed without their community context, omit consideration of what Wilson and Herrnstein (1985) call "communities seen whole," by ignoring "the complex web of interactions in neighborhood settings" (p. 300). Data relating to calls for police service, however, may provide new insight into community concerns, because they are a tangible representation of what community residents want their police to do.

Calls for Service

Calls for police service (CFS data), whether they originate from the 911 emergency communication system or by some other means, can be the source of a great deal of safety-related information. However, in most police departments they have been neglected as a data source for police tactical analysis. As has been described, there are at least three reasons for this, as follows:

- They are too numerous; for example, in 1987 there were over 3 million calls for service received by the CPD, generating over 2 million radio dispatches (and dispatch cards).
- They are not acknowledged as real crime, the presumed primary purpose of police.
- Although the police are required to analyze crime data, there has been little pressure to analyze CFS data.

Although these reasons for neglecting calls for service (vis-a-vis crimes) for tactical planning may have seemed reasonable in the past, they have less validity in an environment in which police response to community concerns takes on greater prominence and in which beat-centered tactical planning can become a reality through the use of mapping.

In fact, mapping facilitates the use of CFS data. In 1987 there were over 113.000 calls for service in District 25. Although this is a considerable number, it averages out to just over one call per hour for each of the district's 12 beats; even if the peak load were four times as great, it would still be manageable. The maps, then, permit the disaggregated data to tell a geographical story.

The fact that incivilities are not considered real crime has much to do with the way police departments are rated in the media (and therefore by the public). The UCR system includes eight crimes as Part I crimes (see footnote 1). It is on these crimes police departments arc generally evaluated whether or not it is appropriate. If the sum of these categories goes up by 10%, then serious crime is said to have gone up by 10%. As we have discussed, community residents are concerned about a whole range of behaviors other than these eight crimes, behaviors that they feel should receive the attention of the police as much as the ones included in the crime statistics. Furthermore, there are indications that the number of disturbance calls in a neighborhood may be a precursor to an increase in the level of Part I crimes. These calls, therefore, may deserve more attention than they currently receive. We made a preliminary analysis of CFS data and found some evidence that disturbance calls may signal an increase in the level of Part I crimes. Although we could not do a longitudinal (or even a cross-sectional) study, such a study should be conducted as a means of determining whether or not data concerning certain incivilities should be routinely collected by police departments.

For the most part, policing has been UCR-driven. Patrol officers are generally told to concentrate on reducing the number of Part I crimes. This means, for example, that an officer may be given more credit for focusing on garage thefts than on reducing the number or duration of disturbances, whereas the community might set the priorities differently. One way to ensure that disturbances are given a higher priority might be to collect statistics on such calls with the same diligence and attention given burglaries. This would mean that there would be increased pressure to analyze CFS data, which may contain a mother lode of useful information that can be mined for a good deal more than crime patterns.

Until very recently, the only research that analyzed CFS data focused on response time. beat structuring (e.g., Hypercube), patrol car allocation (e.g., PCAM). and load shedding (e.g., the Wilmington Split Force experiment). More recently. however. researchers and police administrators have begun to pay more attention to the CFS data to determine the extent to which specific addresses generate repeat complaints or are otherwise police hazards to be noted (Sherman, 1987). Thus, the trend has been to pay more attention to the CFS data, a trend in keeping with the approach taken by the crime mapping research.

Hot Spots

One place in which the CFS data plays a very important role is in the development of community hot spots. The term *hot spot* has long been in use on an informal basis in studies of community crime; in this volume we use the term to denote a location where a number of criminal incidents have taken place or where the community sees a certain danger even though criminal incidents may not have been recorded by the police. In other words, the community and/or police perceive a chronic safety problem at this location. The first use of the term *hot spot* in the formal literature was by Sherman, Gartin, and Buerger, (1989). In this section we review some of the early attempts to study the geographical and ecological aspects of crime.

Attempts to understand the ecology of crime go back to the earliest years of statistics. Geographical and chronological variations in crime and criminal justice first underwent scientific scrutiny by Poisson (Stigler, 1986). In a study of crime in 19th century France, Poisson found a significant difference between the conviction rate in Paris and that in the rest of France;[2] he also compared the conviction rate in Paris for 1830 with that for earlier years and attributed the difference to the revolution of 1830. Subsequent work by Quetelet also addressed the variation in conviction rates but focused more on the study of the average man in different circumstances than on the effect of the variation in environment on the rates (Porter, 1986).

The most well-known and sustained study of the ecology of crime was conducted by the sociologists of the Chicago school of sociology. Park, Burgess, and McKenzie (1925), and later Shaw and McKay (1931, 1969), detailed the great variation in delinquency rates among different communities, attributing the differences to the poverty, inadequate housing, and inadequate opportunities in those areas.

In the past decade there have been a number of studies of the ecological variation in crime. The publications of Jeffery (1971), Newman (1972), Pyle et al. (1974), Harries (1974), Georges-Abeyie and Harries (1980), Brantingham and Brantingham (1981, 1984), Figlio, Hakim, and Rengert (1986), Reiss (1986), and others have described the role that community characteristics, including architecture and traffic patterns, play in the generation and prevention of crime. In an influential article, Cohen and Felson (1979) linked the ecological aspects of crime with the routine activity of an area. More recently, Felson (1987) has suggested how colocation of crime targets and guardians might deter would-be offenders from committing crime; and Harries (1990) shows how maps can assist police in determining how geographic and environmental factors affect crime.

Despite these research efforts, the concept of ecological variation in crime does not appear to have been accepted as a mainstream theoretical construct by many

---

[2]Crime data were not available in France in the 19th century. Studies during this period relied on the statistics collected by courts.

criminologists and sociologists. For example, Stark (1987) decried the fact that much social science research has

lost touch with significant aspects of crime and delinquency. Poor neighborhoods disappeared to be replaced by individual kids with various levels of family income, but no detectable environment at all... Yet through it all, social scientists somehow still knew better than to stroll the streets at night in certain parts of town or even to park there. (p. 844)

Stark urged social science researchers to "reconsider the human ecology approach to deviance." The concept of the hot spot can be considered a response to Stark's exhortation.

A hot spot is not an invariant unit of analysis; for example, Sherman, Gartin. and Buerger (1989) defined it by size (a *place* is defined as "a fixed physical environment which can be seen completely and simultaneously, at least on its surface, by one person's naked eyes") and by activity level (*places* where there were "substantial concentrations of all police calls"–their Table 5 lists 42 hot spots as places that experienced 10 or more predatory crimes in one year). Thus a hot spot has no specific size and no permanent location; if crimes (or calls for service) decrease at that location, then it is no longer a hot spot. Yet it exists nonetheless, as a construct of importance to community residents, who take note of it and avoid it; to police officers, who recognize it by the amount of activity they find there; and to potential investors, who look for more promising areas in which to invest.

While the definition proposed by Sherman et al. readily lends itself to operationalization, it has a number of flaws. First, the hot spot is defined by a specific type of activity, activity that generates calls for police service. There are many other problems (in particular, incivilities) that are considered by community residents to be of the same importance as those represented by CFS data that never reach the police through the 911 emergency telephone system. Second, the definition is year-specific; how this may vary from year to year cannot be investigated. Third, the hot spot is tied to a physical place, and so events that are precipitated by activity at a neighboring place are not considered.

It is readily understandable why this definition contains some of these flaws Sherman et al. were working only with police data, specifically data concerning calls for police service, and they were using only 1 year's data. They state, "Unfortunately, few if any police departments can provide researchers, or even police chiefs, with a year-long call data base ready to analyze." Inclusion of community-generated data provides more insight into community concerns with respect to hot spots.

More important, this definition restricts the size of the hot spot to a place as defined above. Because the activity in one place can be greatly affected by the activity in a nearby place, this restriction appears to be arbitrary. A parallel can be drawn to ecological studies, wherein the unit of analysis depends on the species, the terrain, and the density of predators and prey.

The two different definitions of hot spot may be attributed to the different kinds of community problems focused on by Sherman et al. and by us. The archetypical hot spot found by Sherman et al. might be due to a dysfunctional family (calls relating to child abuse or spouse abuse), or due to a bar (calls relating to fights or disturbing the peace). The archetypical hot spot in our study might be due to (but not solely related to) drug sales in an area that affect the community in other ways, or due to the contiguity of a middle-class area to a rent-subsidized housing project that includes many unsupervised (or poorly supervised) teenagers. Using the Sherman et al. definition, dealing with the specific problem at that location (permanently separating the family members, permanently closing the bar) will cause the hot spot to go away. Using our definition, dealing with the specific problem at that location (arresting dealers and customers, increasing police patrols) will probably just displace it to another location. For the purposes of this volume, we will use our own definition, which is admittedly less precise and more open to interpretation. However, our goal is not to develop quantitative relationships about hot spots but rather to develop an understanding of how they develop and of their effect on a community. A mapping system can be of great benefit in understanding hot spots.

CHAPTER 4

Philosophy Underlying
the Technical Approach

The approach we have taken in implementing the mapping system has been to employ techniques most congenial to the users and to the nature of the data with which they must work. Sometimes this has led to formal quantitative approaches. Often, however, inferences based on an experienced officer's eyeballing of the data to come up with a pattern have been more useful than inferences based on statistical significance.

This chapter first describes the capabilities of the mapping system in its basic form. It then describes the "power-steering" approach to computer use, in which the user does the "driving" (determining how to analyze the data), as distinct from the "autopilot" approach, in which a set of preset algorithms determines what analyses are able to be done.

This ties in with another aspect of our approach, *cognitive data analysis*. This term is used to describe the manner in which an individual will filter data through his or her own experience to infer patterns in the data or to generate hypotheses or conclusions. Although statistical data analysis may be most appropriate in finding patterns of certain types among numerical data, cognitive data analysis may be most appropriate in finding patterns of criminal activity among the available data, which includes offense reports, descriptions of offenders. community activity patterns, land use information, weather, time of day, day of week, month and season of occurrence.

The third aspect of our approach is in the manner of development of the mapping system. Our approach has been to develop it entirely in conjunction with the end users-community organizations as well as the officers and detectives who will have to work with it once the pilot project is over. The principles guiding the development of the system are discussed in the final section of this chapter.

The Basic Mapping System

The advantages of plotting crime on a map over listing crimes are not difficult to understand. By analogy, consider how determining the best route between two cities by either using a map or by using a list of highways that specifies the cities they reach and the highways they intersect. In order to describe the characteristics and advantages of *crime* maps, will we describe the current mapping system that has been developed, which employs commercially available hardware and software.

Figure 4.1 depicts a computer screen used for entering or displaying data for an individual crime.[1] The data are entered by the review officer as part of his or her normal duties (see again Fig. 2.1). Each crime is entered into the data base, with different screens (i.e., different report forms) for different crime types. The data can also be listed as shown in (Fig. 4.2), so that all crimes in a neighborhood can be scanned. However, they can also be depicted collectively on a map as shown in (Fig. 4.3), by locating different symbols (corresponding to different crime types) at their points of occurrence. If, when a map is displayed, more information is desired about a particular crime, the user merely specifies the characteristics of the events to be displayed (see Fig. 4.4), redisplays the map to see which one(s) meet the conditions (see the dark spot in Fig. 4.5), and requests information for this crime (see Fig. 4.6).

There are a number of advantages in using such a system to depict crimes. First, patterns that might not be readily apparent from a list of crimes are readily discernible on a map; for example, in Figure 4.3, the concentration of burglaries near the narcotics hot spot (identified by community organizations) at the intersection of Kildare and Armitage Avenues is striking.

Second, the user has complete flexibility as to what is displayed. The user can determine whether he or she wants to see only burglaries, only crimes committed after dark, only those committed in September, only those committed by juveniles, or all of these. Thus, if a person wants to pursue an idea about a particular crime pattern, whether to identify an offender or to identify a criminogenic condition, the specific crimes suspected of fitting the pattern can be mapped and the idea checked against the data. Although RAMIS can do the same type of search, as was noted in Chapter 2, one of the limitations of the mainframe data base for exploratory analysis is that a person cannot just sit in front of a mainframe console and watch geographic

---

[1]The screen in Figure 4.1 and the maps shown in subsequent figures were developed using the computer package *Business Filevision*, published by Telos Software Products. *Business Filevision* is designed for the Macintosh computer, manufactured by Apple Computer, Inc., and is a graphics system driven by a DBMS. Other hardware and software combinations can also be used; see Appendix B for the desirable characteristics of such a system.

patterns emerge. Also as previously mentioned, CRIMES does not contain the narrative information that is particularly useful for this type of analysis.

Third, geography is incorporated directly into the user's consciousness as the user studies a map as opposed to studying a listing. The effect of railroad tracks and other barriers, as well as the location of schools and commercial establishments, can be seen much more readily when the crime data are mapped.

Computer-drawn maps of a whole city or of sections of a city-showing streets, alleys, and all the details of everyday maps-are now commonplace. Until recently it has been impossible to manipulate graphic information with any but the most expensive and cumbersome equipment. However, because of the development of computer technology and software over the past 5 years, it is now possible for graphic or pictorial information to be displayed and processed with virtually the same ease and flexibility as numeric and text data, and for this information to be made available to the user in any of a variety of forms.

Any information that can be displayed numerically can now be displayed graphically; columns of numbers can be reframed as *business graphics* (pie charts, bar charts, etc.) or as *icons* (symbolic representations of events). Until recently, graphics displays were typically static, single images from which the underlying data could only be recomputed with time-consuming manipulations on expensive equipment. It is now possible to associate graphic information with data bases as flexible and affordable as those associated with numeric and text data, and even to manipulate all of these forms of data within the same data base. Hardware and software considerations are discussed in Appendix B.

Thus, there is the possibility of having different overlays for depicting different types of information in much the same way that transparent overlays can be used on printed maps. On a computer it is possible to overlay the basic geography with varieties of other information-for example, buildings and other properties can be shaded or color-coded according to type of land use-or with bus stops and bus routes.

The Power Steering versus the Autopilot Approach

We have termed our approach to the use of computers the *power steering approach*, as distinct from the *autopilot approach*. In using an autopilot approach, the means of analysis are preset and available to the user at the touch of a button. An autopilot approach is appropriate whenever standard analyses are to be performed repeatedly. If routine analyses of the data are frequently required (e.g., a breakdown of robberies by age and sex of offender and by location type), then such a procedure can be automatically programmed to be generated.

When analyses are made for tactical purposes or to study one-shot phenomena on an ad hoc basis (e.g., analyzing a specific pattern of offenses that have just cropped up in one particular district), then the autopilot approach is of much less benefit. Unless the standard analyses include every possible way to analyze the data, then it is best to permit the crime analyst to develop his or her own repertoire of analyses based on intuition and experience.

Under the power steering approach the end user-not the computer program or systems analyst–determines how the computer is to be driven to perform analyses. In a parallel development, (Waldrop 1989), the new philosophy of aircraft automation more closely resembles the power steering approach than the autopilot approach because overly computerized cockpits promote too much passivity in pilots: "It means putting automation back on the right track: as an assistant to the pilots" (p. 1533). Rather than being provided with a limited repertoire of possible analytic or graphical techniques, the user is encouraged to plot or analyze the data in any way he or she sees fit. This is most useful in cases in which standard analyses are deficient, that is, in which patterns may chance from offender to offender, day to day, or location to location. This is certainly the case in the analysis of crime patterns.

An example may clarify this point. Most studies of the geographical context of crime, including the Spatial and Temporal Analysis of Crime (STAC) project of the Illinois Criminal Justice Information Authority described in Chapter 2, employ statistical techniques for analyzing the data. One of their products is a set of computer algorithms for analyzing spatial-temporal clustering of crimes. However useful these algorithms might be, they ignore the relationship between the underlying patterns of crime and the social context giving rise to crime, an understanding of which can be obtained from community residents, from information about incivilities, and from information about local conditions known by local residents and beat officers. This social context information cannot be easily factored into computer algorithms.

Suppose that between 10:30 and 11:00 on a Friday night four calls for service are received by a police department, all within a mile of each other: a street robbery, an attempted break-in, a smash-and-grab, and a gang fight. In a traditionally organized police department like Chicago's, they would be handled by four different officers (perhaps from different districts). Any follow-up would probably be handled by different detectives with different areas of specialization, so it is likely that no connection would be made between the incidents during the follow-up investigation.

Suppose that the incidents are then depicted on a map that shows a high school right in the center of these incidents, and it is known (or even better, portrayed on the map) that the high school basketball game let out at 10:20 that Friday night.[2] In this case the social context that relates these four seemingly unrelated calls for service could in no way be factored into a computer algorithm, yet to the analyst the pattern stands out clearly.

It would not be worthwhile to create a pattern search algorithm to account for this relationship. The algorithm would be irrelevant in most cases and would waste

---

[2]In the case of basketball games and other such scheduled events, a district commander is of course aware of the potential for disturbance following the game and would deploy patrol officers accordingly. The situation described is a hypothetical one.

computer storage space and processing time–one can envision devising specialized algorithms for so many special cases that they eventually clog the computer's arteries. Furthermore, a pattern search algorithm would be useful for some police districts and not for others where some other focal point (a transportation hub, a shopping. center. a tavern) might be a major generator of crime or calls for service. With regard to transit crime, for example, Wachs (1989) points out that "the magnitude of transit crime is understated by crime reporting mechanisms. Uniform crime reporting forms do not designate transit stations or vehicles as specific venues for recording crimes, and they are thus lumped together with many other crimes in a category called 'street crimes... (p.1548). This is not quite correct; most cities, including Chicago, have special location codes that specify whether or not a crime took place on public transit vehicles or property. However, a street location code would ordinarily be given if a crime occurred while the victim was waiting for a bus on the street or a block or two away after exiting a transit vehicle. This would tend to mask the transit-related aspect of the crime, but a map-based crime analysis system would be able to spot this relationship.

Because of the differences among districts and different aspects of crimes, we feel that to be most effective, a computer-based mapping system should be decentralized and customized to the needs of the particular area. This makes the district police more responsive to changing circumstances within their district, as well as to the particular needs of the community organizations within their jurisdiction. This is particularly important for a large urban police department such as the CPD, whose jurisdiction covers such a heterogeneous mix of neighborhoods, each with unique challenges for the police. It also makes it possible for the police district to handle short-term fluctuations in the demand for different police services. It is for this reason, too, that a power steering approach implemented on a personal computer, or a desktop computer, or a computer work station appears to be the most promising way to design the mapping system. Of course, the crime data collection should be centralized and stored on the mainframe computer. But the districts and other units should have the ability to analyze its data without having to tie up the mainframe.

There is no technical reason that power steering cannot be programmed onto a mainframe computer; however, it is too costly. Making speculative runs while looking for tactical patterns may not be possible. However, a crime analyst using a microcomputer can perform such analyses without having, to request assistance from the relatively few who know how to use the mainframe software.

A microcomputer-based approach would also make it easier to share information with others. Whereas a community organization may have access to a microcomputer (some Chicago community organizations have their own) and can be given a disk containing crime and incivility information pertaining to their community, sharing such information using a mainframe is much more difficult. As noted earlier, CANS has been obtaining a tape of crime data from the CPD's mainframe. However, it uses another mainframe to download the relevant data to floppy disks for delivery to community organizations. This operation is expensive and time-consuming compared to a direct micro-to-floppy disk transfer.

Unlike centralized, mainframe-based systems, a microcomputer-based approach encourages decentralization and customization to the needs of the particular area. More important from the standpoint of the power steering approach, the greater access to a microcomputer-based system encourages experimentation, curiosity, and speculation concerning potential patterns in the data.

Cognitive Data Analysis

Computerized data analysis normally refers to the use of statistical routines to analyze data to see if trends and patterns can be inferred. The data can be analyzed using a number of different statistical packages; as mentioned earlier, in the CPD the data are analyzed using RAMIS. The primary technique used to analyze crime data is cross-tabulation of the data. The results are often presented in voluminous computer printouts to be pored over by the users.

Such analyses are useful when dealing with patterns that are easy to extract from the data or have in some way been anticipated by the data collection process. For example, it is easy to investigate patterns by time of day, day of week, or type of crime, because these data elements are all entered into the CRIMES data base. It is much more difficult to use CRIMES to investigate patterns that refer to geographical characteristics, such as the distance from an armed commercial robbery to an expressway entrance or from a purse snatching to a subway entrance.

Of course, it is possible to enter such data elements into the CRIMES data base by requiring the responding officer to note the relevant distances on the offense report form. But even contemplating, this move shows how senseless it would be. Although the cited distances may be important in a few cases of armed commercial robbery or purse snatching, they would be a waste of the responding officer's time in the vast majority of cases.

However, the geographical context of an offense may furnish an understanding as to why and how the crime took place, and how it might be prevented. It is for this reason that most field detectives are geographically based and have a tendency to specialize so that they can investigate similar cases and, based on their memory and their personal "data base"–their memories and their paper files of case reports–try to distinguish contextual features that might be useful in identifying the offender or preventing further crimes of the same nature. (See Chapter 7 for more on the use of information by detectives.)

A data base management system that includes a map of the incidents can incorporate a great deal of contextual information about the portrayed offenses. Not only does it show the geographical relationships among the incidents, but it also permits the analyst to consider other relationships that might have generated the incidents (or a subset of them), such as the relationship between land use and crime; the relationship between time of day and type of offense; and joint relationships, such as those between certain types of offenses committed in some types of areas at certain times.

Such a system is not only useful in *testing* hypotheses about patterns of crime (e.g., testing to see if most robberies of dry cleaning, establishments take place in the evening); more important, it is useful in *generating* hypotheses about patterns of crime. In the example described in the previous section, it was the crime analyst's knowledge about the possible aftermath of a high school basketball game that tied a robbery, a break-in. a smash-and-grab, and a gang fight together. In this case a hypothesis was generated about the underlying pattern that could not possibly be pulled out of a purely statistics-oriented data base management system. Our approach is similar with respect to crime data to the one championed by Tukey (1977) for data of all kinds: Explore the data, preferably using graphical means. to see if patterns emerge.

Crime mapping, therefore, adds a new dimension to the repertoire of crime analysts. It permits them to use information that has been collected for decades but has been largely unavailable to them because of the difficulties in combining the different types of data. Analysts can combine information that could not be combined heretofore and can use the collective experience of the department to generate hypotheses rather than relying entirely on their own memory and their own experience to infer patterns from the data. This new dimension, which we have termed *cognitive data analysis*, simultaneously permits and promotes sharing of information among different units within a police department and, as will be shown, between the police and community organizations as well.

This type of analysis has much in common with artificial intelligence and expert systems approaches. The primary difference between our approach and these others is that we do not expect an expert system to replace human analysts; we are dealing with a much broader range of patterns than do most expert systems. When using an expert system for medical diagnosis, for example, the user expects to find the same general symptoms in everyone with a given disease; for example. people with jaundice almost always have a yellow pallor. When dealing with crime patterns, however, there is no reason to assume that the crime patterns generated by one person should be replicated by another person: some burglars may always enter through a basement window, but others do not. Although the *approach* a crime analyst uses to develop the pattern may be similar from offender to offender, the *behaviors* that are studied are not similar.

User-Based System Development

The development work for the crime mapping project took into consideration not only the hardware and software aspects of the system but the social and organizational features as well, reflecting a concern for interpersonal relationships and organizational infrastructure that would promote joint efforts among individuals in different organizations. Based on our experience in previous projects, and on the early phases of this project, the mapping system has been designed according to the following precepts.

The system should be developed in consultation with the users. The response we have received again and again suggests that the system we developed was more fully appreciated and utilized by the users because it was a joint effort. The following are four reasons for developing, a system jointly with its users:

- Imposed systems inevitably come with an "us versus them" quality that sets a bad tone for an ongoing relationship.
- The primary users must not be intimidated by the technology and must be sufficiently acquainted with the computer to deal with the day-to-day questions and glitches that inevitably occur.
- A jointly developed system can be personalized in a way that makes it easier for the user to appreciate and understand; moreover, the user then knows how to revise and adapt it even further if necessary.
- The system is inevitably better than it would be otherwise because of the mutual insights provided by the cooperating parties.

In addition, the production of the system itself provides an occasion for the parties to develop a stronger working, relationship and to learn from each other.

The system should provide timely, easily understood information. Information that arrives too late or is almost incomprehensible to the intended audience is not worth the time taken to provide it. Users become discouraged and feel more burdened than they did without the system. The maps should not confuse the user; rather, they should allow the user to understand information in ways that were previously impossible. This means that the system should allow the user to display many types of events, should use pictorial representations that are relatively self-explanatory, and should allow for easy visual distinctions between different events.

The system should provide information at the local level. One aspect of the power steering approach is to have the information available at the level where it will do the most good–at the district level for managerial purposes and at the beat level for use by beat officers. Because the district commander has ultimate responsibility for the safety of the district, he or she should have direct access to it. For the same reason, beat-level information should be provided to beat officers.

The system should require minimal additional police resources. Most users, especially the police, feel overburdened by the tasks they already are required to accomplish. This is especially true with respect to filling out additional reports or entering additional data. To the extent that additional data or time is required, particularly as an add-on to present efforts, the system will be resisted.

The system should display information on an as-requested basis. Inevitably the information that accumulates in maps or reports soon overwhelms the user; its density (and irrelevance) can be so discouraging that the system is no longer used or useful. The user must have substantial control over the data to be displayed and analyzed.

The system should accommodate a wide variety of reports and maps The reports that are required routinely should be prepared with as few keystrokes as possible. However, special reports should not be beyond the ability of the user.

The system should support the maps with other data. To the extent to which the maps or any output formats do not speak for themselves, the user must be able to obtain the details to augment the graphic output.

The system should permit data confidentiality to be maintained. If confidentiality is unattainable, the system will be avoided or its purpose will be distorted; little information of value will be entered. But control over access will encourage use. For example, the exact addresses of crime locations on the data maps and reports provided to community groups are not given, so that individual addresses are held confidential; this was designed into the systems and procedures we developed for provision of data and maps to community organizations.

The philosophy underlying the user-based development environment outlined above manifests itself in many aspects of the crime mapping project. In general, the project members have attempted to take into account the social and organizational context in which they were working in each phase and to work with personnel in designing, implementing, and assessing, the work. This way of proceeding has been congenial and is consonant with their work in several other projects.

However, there are practical as well as philosophical reasons for this approach. The literature on human organization has increasingly come to emphasize the importance of the full cooperation of workers if project goals are to be achieved. Our use in this project of the power steering metaphor not only took advantage of the experience and skills of police personnel, but also helped them buy in to the work and its satisfactory implementation. The adoption of a user-friendly interface on the computer implementation not only made the system easier to use and cut down dramatically on the training time required, but also welcomed the participants by showing them that additional effort had been taken to make the system useful. Careful consideration of the community and its interests enlarges the number of informed people who have invested in understanding, and improving the community crime problem; to the extent that these people bring new bodies of knowledge they can be especially productive participants (Bush & Gordon, 1982). Also, the combined participation of police and community residents using information, equipment, and approaches that they find mutually beneficial has had the additional advantage of cutting into the layers of mistrust that had built up over the years. In short, these humanizing efforts, despite the extra effort they required in the early stages, paid off in numerous ways in the long run.

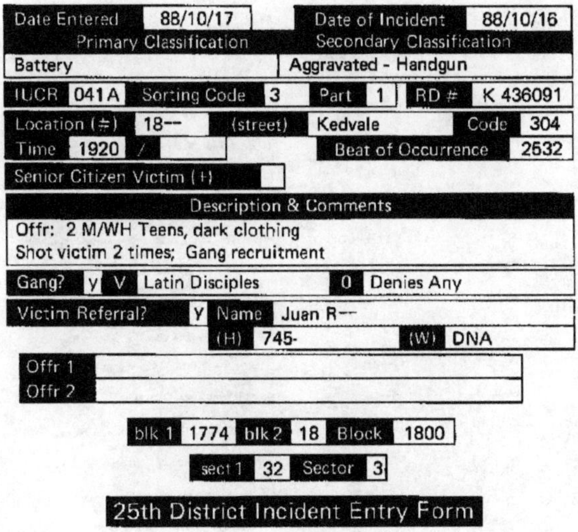

Date Entered	88/10/17		Date of Incident	88/10/16

Primary Classification	Secondary Classification
Battery	Aggravated - Handgun

IUCR	041A	Sorting Code	3	Part	1	RD #	K 436091

Location (#)	18--	(street)	Kedvale	Code	304

Time 1920 /   Beat of Occurrence   2532

Senior Citizen Victim (+)

Description & Comments
Offr: 2 M/WH Teens, dark clothing
Shot victim 2 times; Gang recruitment

Gang?   y   V   Latin Disciples   0   Denies Any

Victim Referral?   Y   Name   Juan R--

(H)   745-   (W)   DNA

Offr 1

Offr 2

blk 1   1774   blk 2   18   Block   1800

sect 1   32   Sector   3

25th District Incident Entry Form

Figure 4.1. Computer screen displaying
individual crime record

When	What	Where	Who & What
/ 4700	Criminal Sex Assault	67—North [2537] K 415910	
/ 1700	Vehicle Theft	17—Kostner K 405880	
	Robbery	19—Liciva K 428039	
88/09/16 1000 / 3700	Burglary Unlawful Entry	37—Wabansia K 403600	Entry was made in unknown manner. Loss at this time 1 V set.
88/09/16 2300 / 1900	Burglary Four Side Entry	19—Lowell K 400082	Entry was made thru side door of garage. Loss at this time M set. tools.
88/09/17 1725 / 4400	Theft Purse Snatching	44—North K 407758	Offender or redhair reaches out and grabbed victims purse NFC.
88/09/18 1100 / 1900	Burglary Unlawful Entry	19—Rutgers K 410104	Entry was made in unknown manner. Loss at this time VCR
88/09/19 1300 / 1800	Burglary Forcible Entry	14—Monticello K 417288	Entry was made thru window of apartment. Loss at this time, VCR.
1400 3700	Vehicle Theft	37—Armitage K 410223	LAD47011 85 19/81 Ford Mustang, red in color
1900 / 1700	Vehicle Theft	17—Kostner K 411278	V2991 ILL 84 1978 Olds Delta White in color
2000 . 4400	Vehicle Theft	44—Grand K 411754	BHM148 ILL 86 1964 Chev. 2dr. Silver in color
88/09/20 0001 / 1700	Vehicle Theft	17—Tripp K 412340	LM1886 ILL 85 1978 Olds Cutlass Maroon in color
1300 / 1600	Vehicle Theft	28—Pulaski K 412847	116574 ILL 86 1984 Honda Motorcycle
88/09/21 0100 / 1300	Vehicle Theft	16—Lacero K 413691	724425 ILL 1981 Pont. 4dr. Brown in color.
0325 / 1700	Robbery Strong Arm	17—Cicero K 413828	Offender 1 M/B 30-40 5/06 Offender took USC from victim
0900 . 2000	Burglary Forcible Entry	20—Kostner K 415114	Entry was made thru front door of apartment. Loss at this time. Men's jewelry.
0000 1600	Burglary Forcible Entry	19—Tripp K 415149	Entry was made thru front door of apartment. Loss at this time. Several supplies.
1800 · 1700	Robbery Strong Arm	17—Kostner K 415050	Offender 2 M/B No further description. Offender took USC from victim
1900 1600	Burglary Forcible Entry	16—Pulaski K 415078	Entered by forced door. 4402 Loss.
88/09/22 1700 1000	Burglary Unlawful Entry	19—Lowell K 415462	Entry was made in unknown manner. Loss at this time 1978 More no lic plates.
88/09/23 1630 · 1700	Robbery Armed Armed B arr	17—Tripp K 415608	Victim refused to identify himself after reporting that someone tried to rob him. No descriptions.
88/09/24 0900 / 1400	Vehicle Theft	17—Pulaski K 419721	State Plates Applied For. 83 Cadillac DeVille 2dr Silver
2100 / 1700	Vehicle Theft	17—Keeler K 418322	SIPM 857 ILL 86 Olds Cutlass 4dr Gray.
2145 / 4100	Robbery Armed Knife	41—North K 420200	1 M/b 25-30, 8ft, 185 lbs, Blue hooded sweat shirt & jeans. Offender took money and stamps from victim

| Main Report | Page 1 | | A courteous police officer is a happy police officer |

Figure 4.2. Computer screen for displaying
crime data in a listed format

When	What	Where	Who & What
88/09/25 2200 / 1900	Burglary Unlawful Entry	19 — Central Park 2532 K 427340	Garage door. Offender(s) took miscellaneous auto tools. Motor stand, Radio and Battery charger.
88/09/26 0400 / 3900	Vehicle Theft	39 — Armitage K 423167	None 1983 Ford 4dr. White in color.
88/09/27 1000 / 3700	Vehicle Theft	37 — Wabansia K 425171	None 1979 Pont. 2dr Blue in color.
2200 / 4000	Burglary Unlawful Entry	40 — Wabansia K 425712	Entry was made in unknown manner Loss at this time. Kitchen sinks.
88/09/28 0800 / 1600	Vehicle Theft	16 — Tripp K 425169	None 1979 Chev. 4dr. Black in color.

Beat of Occurence Count:
                      29

Overall Count:
                      29

Figure 4.2. continued

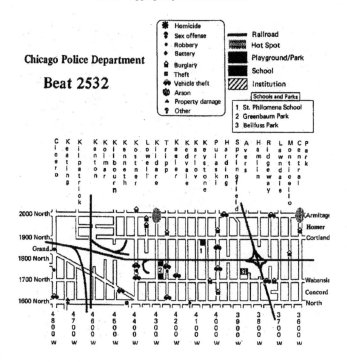

Figure 4.3. Computer screen displaying
crime data on a map.

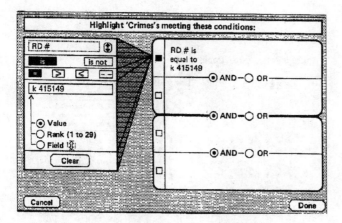

Figure 4.4. Computer screen allowing user to
specify characteristics of crimes to be displayed.

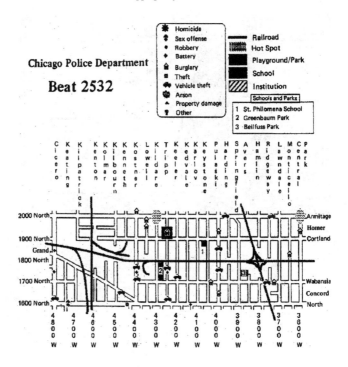

Figure 4.5 Computer screen displaying
map with specified crime highlighted.

Date Entered	88/09/22		Date of incident	88/09/21

Primary Classification	Secondary Classification
Burglary	Forcible Entry

IUCR	0610	Sorting Code	5	Part	1	RD #	K 415149

Location (#)	1927	(street)	Tripp		Code
Beat of Occurrence	2532	Time	0900		290
Senior Citizen (+)		/	1900		

Description & Comments

Entry was made thru window of apartment. Loss at this time. School supplies.

Gang?	V		0

Victim Referral?		Name	
		(H)	(W)

Data Entry Form

Blk 1	1877	Block	1900
Blk 2	19		

Figure 4.6. Computer screen giving details
of highlighted crime.

Part II
Using the Maps

The mapping system was implemented at two sites within the CPD. Basically, the system was the same one that had been used in CANS and its affiliated community organizations to display the crime data provided by the CPD. The difference between the community implementations and the CPD implementations, however, was that the data provided to the CPD were more timely and more complete exact addresses and a description of the event, the victim(s), and the offender(s) were included in the data base.

Part II describes the manner in which the two CPD units were selected for implementing the system as well as the results of using the maps in these units. In particular, it discusses how individual patrol and tactical officers used the beat maps, how detectives used district maps, how management of patrol resources was facilitated using the maps, and how the maps were used cooperatively by the police and community organizations.

Part II is based on observations by the research team of patrol and detective operations, as well as on intensive interviews with more than 60 patrol and tactical officers, detectives, and command personnel. We also observed community organizations and interviewed their members. By observing and asking questions about the nature of police work, their reactions to the crime mapping system, and their suggestions for improving it, we were able to obtain useful information on how the mapping system affected both police operations and the relationship between the police and the community.

CHAPTER 5

Selection of Units for
Project Implementation

Two units within the CPD were chosen as sites for implementation of the project. Because the project's goals relate to inferring patterns by mapping crime and community data on computer- generated maps, one of the units selected was a patrol district and another was a unit within the detective division that could take advantage of crime mapping. This chapter describes the manner in which the selection of units was made and the results of the implementations.

Selecting a Patrol District

The specific district was not selected until the project was started, although the following criteria were proposed: It was to be a district that had more than the average crime rate and one in which there was at least one community organization affiliated with CANS. We were all mindful, however, that for such a project to work the district commander would need to be receptive to its implementation in his or her district. We were going to be developing a concept that we felt would work in a variety of circumstances, but for the same reason that new airplanes are flown first by test pilots with greater flying skills than the run-of-the-mill pilots who eventually fly the plane, we wanted the experimental district to be piloted by a commander who not only would not be threatened or intimidated by innovation but would also attempt to put the mapping system through its paces and see what it could do.

The actual selection of the district was made by the CPD, with the advice of the other project parties. A number of candidate districts were suggested, but the one that was eventually selected by the CPD was the unanimous choice of all parties. District 25, located on the West Side, had a substantial crime rate. In 1987, there were 14,257 index crimes; 80,703 miscellaneous noncriminal incidents; and 8,950 non-index crimes in District 25. There were also 113,720 calls for service, which was 4.7% of the total calls for service in the city. Many of the communities within its borders had experienced and continue to experience a high population turnover, the newcomers generally having lower incomes than those who leave. District 25 also has an organized citizenry, with more than 70 community organizations or block clubs within or partially within its borders. More to the point, within District 25 are three community organizations affiliated with CANS, a larger number than in any other district. Fortunately, the district commander was very receptive to this project.

We had originally anticipated that the research would be conducted off-line, using stale data, just to see how the mapping project could be translated into a workable one for the CPD and other police departments. What occurred was somewhat unsettling, especially to those on the project team who were used to conducting research under controlled conditions testing and evaluating each component before incorporating the next component. Instead, the rapid pace with which this project began was exciting and exhilarating; the district commander *integrated it fully into his operation within 1 week of its introduction into the district.*

The rapid implementation of the mapping system into District 25 was facilitated by the very real problems of data entry in the CPD–and, as we have since learned, in virtually every large police department in the country. For example, the Los Angeles Police Department (1988) describes its system as consisting of

a slow, cumbersome series of manual tasks. The system is inefficient and negatively impacts the overall effectiveness by wasting valuable officer time: not providing needed information in a timely manner; and not providing a data base with the accuracy, speed, and information necessary for the development of advanced investigative systems... Delays are more the rule rather than the exception in the current reporting system ... As a result, this information is not available to either officers or detectives on a timely basis. Detectives often receive arrest reports so late that there is insufficient time to do a thorough investigation before a suspect is due to be released, and detectives are sometimes unaware of other crimes the suspect may have also committed. (pp. 5-6)

As described in Chapter 2, the district commander relies on the 24-hour activity report, prepared by the review officer on a daily basis for learning what has been going on in the district. The 24-hour activity report became the data-gathering vehicle for this project as well. Using it allowed us not only to obtain the necessary data but also to do so with two major advantages:

1. No additional work was necessary for the officers, because they typed the same data into the computer instead of on the typewriter. In fact, the workload decreased somewhat after the officers got used to the computer because of the ease of correcting typographical mistakes.
2. By allowing officers to work with up-to-date data, the project immediately became involved in day-to-day operations. In effect, this permitted us to gauge the effectiveness of the mapping system without the constraints and unrealistic assumptions that working off-line would have required.

Thus, we were able to use existing CPD manual data collection procedures to provide the data for the mapping system. However, this opportunity was not without its costs. The rapid integration of the mapping system made it impossible to conduct a step-by-step implementation of the project, one that would permit a careful evaluation. Instead, we found ourselves working more closely with operational, day-to-day problems. The enthusiasm of the commander and his analysis officer, however, and the ability to develop so many results so quickly more than compensated for the costs. Furthermore, the community groups were able to obtain data from the district with a shorter turnaround time as well, which created enthusiasm for the project from another direction.

Selecting a Detective Unit

In our initial project plan, we specified that we would focus on the crime analysis unit (CAU), a central unit located within the detective division (as described in Chapter 2). One of its primary tasks is to review all felony incidents and generate crime pattern bulletins. (See Appendix C for the detective division special order relating to this task.)

As can be seen from the special order, the focus of the crime pattern bulletin is on the *offender*. The assumption that the nonpolice members of the project team held of the aims and interests of the crime analysis unit–which was that the CAU focuses on geographic-based patterns–was incorrect from the start. The CAU's primary concern is generating lists of offenses that are attributable to a given offender or group of offenders. Patterns of this sort have legal implications because they may be challenged in court. Therefore, they are purposely aimed at specific offenders and tend to be conservative (i.e., to err on the side of exclusion rather than inclusion). Pointing out hot spots is of secondary importance to this unit; General information bulletins are the vehicle whereby this information is disseminated.

Thus, we determined that the CAU was not the optimal location for implementing a mapping system. We therefore began to explore the possibility of implementing the system in another unit in the detective division. The building that houses District 25 also houses the detective unit for Area 5, which is comprised of Districts 14, 15, 16, 17, and 25. When the project started in District 25, personnel from the Area 5 detective unit heard our presentations and saw the computer system demonstrated. They were interested in what the system could do for them and enthusiastically volunteered to be a test site. Because no computer was available for use by these detectives, they at first shared use of the District 25 computer. The district workload, however, increased as more and more functions previously done by hand were done by computer. This effectively prevented Area 5 detectives from making full use of the mapping system until the first half of 1988, when they borrowed a Macintosh for 5 months. This made it possible for us to report on a partial implementation of the crime mapping project in a detective field unit as well as in a district.

Implementation in District 25

The mapping system, which we named MAPADS, was completely implemented in District 1 25 and used daily, having been integrated into the district's operational routine.[1] By completely integrated, we mean that:

- computerized beat maps for all beats in the district were provided and revised as necessary;
- as described earlier, a source of up-to-date crime data was identified, as well as a means of entering the data without the need for additional resources;
- technical assistance was provided to the district as needed; and
- a procedure was developed for placing icons on the map by CANS, one that relieved the district from having to perform this very time-consuming task.[2]

This last point needs additional explanation. The software we were using did not have the capability of translating an address into an x-y coordinate, and then placing the appropriate icon (e.g.. a picture of a car for an auto theft) at the x-y coordinate where it occurred. To accomplish this task for the 50 or so incidents each day would have taken a few hours of a police officer's time. During the project, the data were sent to CANS. Initially this was done by sending a disk from District 25 to headquarters, where a CANS staff member would pick it up; later the data were transmitted electronically. CANS personnel placed the icons on the maps, and returned the data to District 25.

The need to place each icon manually on the map had a deleterious effect on the project. Although the offense data were typed into the computer daily, they were originally unavailable for use on the maps for more than a week. The reason for this was the transportation delay in getting the data to CANS and back. First. it was decided that it was not useful to send a diskette each day to CANS for its staff to use to place the icons on the map. This would have meant a steady stream of diskettes going from District 25 to CPD headquarters. from there to CANS offices. and back again. Furthermore, a trial run made it clear that the volume was too low to reveal patterns and thereby justify the effort. Eventually, the data were instead sent weekly,

[1]Although the crime mapping project ended in June of 1988, District 25 continued to use MAPADS well beyond that time, without the support of the research team.

[2]This procedure, which included the transmission of data from one site to another. should
not be necessary in the future. New software packages, developed in part based on the project's specifications (see Appendix B), eliminate the need for manual placement of icons.

then biweekly, to CANS. After a CANS staff member placed the icons on the map, the diskette was returned to District 25 by way of CPD headquarters (see Fig. 5.1).

Despite the delays, the crime mapping project served as a major step forward in patrol-based tactical analysis. As discussed earlier, the professionalism and expertise of the CPD personnel contributed greatly to the successful implementation of MAPADS. The project found several officials in key positions in the CPD who were both computer literate and enthusiastic. This factor was a key ingredient in the project's swift adoption in District 25 as well as in the detective division.

A second advantage the project enjoyed was the reputation and working relationships its component organizations had already established. CANS and NU had long worked together to make municipal information useful and available to community organizations under NU's Affirmative Neighborhood Information Program (ANIP).[3] UIC had a strong and ongoing relationship with the CPD, specifically in terms of exchanges of personnel and representation on advisory committees. In addition, the principal investigators at UIC and NU had worked together in the past. Thus, the constituent organizations entered the scene with relationships that helped to bridge the gap that had initially separated the CPD and CANS.

In short, the crime mapping project had a lot going for it from its inception. To understand the success of this effort and contemplate diffusion of the innovation to other units and police departments, it is essential to keep the need for developing strong working relationships in mind and to plan implementation accordingly.

Implementation in Area 5

Area detectives are charged with the investigation and follow-up of crimes in geographic areas. They focus more on individuals whose offense patterns are restricted geographically; furthermore, they are more on the spot when it comes to making arrests and thus have a strong incentive to use whatever means available to do so. In fact, Area 5 detectives committed a great deal of their own resources to the crime mapping project, assigning two detectives part-time to data entry and analysis. They were confident that the system would help them track offender and offense patterns more readily. To this end, project personnel manually drew computer-based maps of all five districts in Area 5, for use by Area 5 detectives.[4] After familiarizing

---

[3]Aside from providing crime data to community organizations, ANIP also provided monthly reports to community organizations concerning buildings in housing court (a task since taken over by the City of Chicago Planning Department) and economic development projects.

[4]This is another example of a step that will probably not be necessary in the future. The existence of digital map files produced by the U.S. Census Bureau and others means that the maps can be purchased by a police department that is developing a mapping system at the same time it purchases the mapping hardware and software (see Appendix B).

themselves with the mapping system and being provided with maps of the districts in Area 5, detectives in the Area 5 violent crimes unit began to enter robbery data into the computer on January 1, 1988.

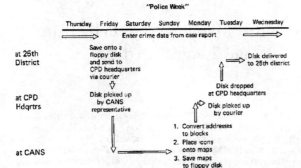

Figure 5.1. Data journey for icon placement
in MAPADS.

CHAPTER 6

Use of the Mapping System by Patrol and Tactical Officers

The crime mapping research project was primarily concerned with conceptualizing, developing, and refining MAPADS as a system for use by police. Thus, it was not also possible to perform a formal evaluation of its capabilities. yet we do have strong indications of the benefits of MAPADS for patrol and tactical use. In order to explain the way in which the mapping system was used by patrol and tactical officers, this chapter describes the way they were assigned to anticrime patrols prior to the advent of the mapping system. A number of typical examples of MAPADS' use are then given, showing how patrol deployment has been affected by MAPADS. This chapter then describes one of the most important benefits of MAPADS in police patrol-its use as a beat's memory.

Pre-MAPADS Patrol and Tactical Allocation

Before the mapping system was incorporated into the operations of District 25, patrol and tactical officers were given directed patrol assignments based primarily on crime statistics. That is, if a series of robberies was discovered, for instance. based on the monthly statistical breakdowns provided to the district by the data systems division. then the beat officers would be apprised of the situation; in addition, a directed patrol mission might be prepared for the tactical unit for appropriate enforcement action.

These assignments were made by the district commander or other command personnel. Even the best patrol officers may not notice a pattern in their own beats; as discussed later in this chapter, patrol officers cannot easily track the extent of criminal and other antisocial activity on their beats. Furthermore, even if they saw a problem accumulating on their beats, some of the officers we interviewed said that they might be reluctant to inform their superior officers for the following reasons: they might have to write a report about it, which is anathema to most officers; they might be considered too gung ho by their fellow officers; and there is in ethic among some police officers akin to that among soldiers of, "Don't volunteer for anything." This, of course, does not hold true for all officers we interviewed and especially not for tactical officers. It does point out, however, one of the obstacles to implementation of MAPADS in the CPD and other departments. For these reasons, the statistical summary of crimes provided by CPD headquarters was the primary mechanism for allocating discretionary patrol resources, such as for directed patrol missions. District commanders are limited in their ability to redirect patrol resources because of the constraint that all beats be covered. However, tactical officers and the multibeat sector cars have more mobility and can be directed to trouble spots. In addition, MAPADS helped direct patrol officers within their beats.

Another mechanism for resource allocation was based on analyses of a more informal nature. The district commander and other district command personnel read the 24-hour activity report every day. They used their own memory and experience to spot patterns and hot spots developing in their districts. Based on their own assessment of the situation they would divert resources to those locations.

A third mechanism for resource allocation was based on external pressures. If an incident made the headlines or if a community organization brought what it considered to be a dangerous or disruptive situation to the attention of the district commander, then additional patrol and tactical resources would be allocated to that particular situation for as long as it appeared to be warranted.

If a car was given a particular assignment (e.g., auto theft or purse snatching), the officers would go to the review office, where all case reports are stored, and manually go through the files and read the relevant reports on all such crimes within the past month. In this way they would try to assimilate all of the information about the crimes. If no pattern emerged readily from their review of the case reports, the officers would have no clear direction or strategy to pursue.

Specific Examples of MAPADS Use

Within District 25, geographically based crime analysis using the mapping system has been shown to have a number of benefits. The following examples are typical:[1]

---

[1]We feel that a great number of uses of MAPADS may be unreported. For example, in an informal discussion about the maps during a graduate class taught by one of the project staff, a student (who happens to be a beat officer in District 25) described how she received a map showing a number of thefts from garages in a certain area of her beat. She and her partner then began checking garage doors in the area and found one that had been jimmied. A little patience was subsequently rewarded by the arrest of two burglars. Would this have been possible without MAPADS? The student said no. Did she report this successful use of MAPADS to her superior officer? "No, it's not worth the extra paperwork." she said.

• A patrol officer on a foot beat on North Avenue kept a crime history of his beat by retaining copies of maps produced by MAPADS. These maps showed the officer a concentration of strong-arm (smash-and-grab) robberies in a two-block stretch of his beat. A little research on his part and discussions with the local merchants revealed that the robberies were occurring after dark and that the overhead street lights for the area were continually being tampered with by the local youths. The officer contacted the district commander, and the following steps were taken: A crime awareness bulletin was prepared (see Fig. 6.1) for all relevant personnel in District 25. The appropriate city officials were contacted, and they promised to get the lights back on and make them tamper-proof. A crime analysis pattern was subsequently issued by the CAU. The pattern was later cleared by arrest, and the officer was given an honorable mention for his efforts. This points out one ramification of the MAPADS system, especially when used in conjunction with problem- oriented policing-a recognition of the accomplishments in the reward structure for officers. It is unusual for a patrol officer to be given recognition for contacting city agencies. For MAPADS and POP to be effectively implemented, however, changes in the reward structure may be necessary. In Houston, for example (Dodenhoff, 1989), the assistant chief noted that

police officers have been doing for a long time many of the things that we're now asking them to do. It's just that there's been no formalization of that. They've never gotten credit for doing it, and it was never considered important. They know it was important, because that's the stuff they dealt with every day. So they did a lot of it on the sly while they were doing all the things we thought we wanted them to do, like writing traffic tickets and things like that... It's management changing, not patrolmen changing.

• The Hermosa Community Organization is affiliated with the Northwest Neighborhood Federation, one of the member organizations of CANS. After an increase in crime, the residents of this neighborhood established the Hermosa Anti-Crime Committee. The committee met with the District 25 neighborhood relations sergeant and expressed their strong concern about the crime situation. Specifically, they were concerned with the apparent proliferation of gang and narcotics activity. The crime analysis officer, using MAPADS, prepared maps and reports showing the actual hot spots, and meetings were held with the district commander, other command personnel, and the superintendent of police. Citizens expressed their fears, which were allayed by showing them the actual crime level on the maps. This permitted the discussion to focus on actual problem areas, which were jointly identified and targeted through the creation of a police task force to concentrate enforcement activities in the hot spot areas. Uniformed patrols were increased as well. Continued communication between the community and the department permitted the district to tailor the police resources to address the expressed concerns. Follow-up analysis revealed a reduction in crime, and follow-up communication with community residents revealed a reduction in fear of crime.

• A tactical officer started working on the day shift and wanted to know where the daytime burglaries were concentrated. The district's crime analysis officer produced a map showing the locations (see Fig. 6.2); the officer and his partner began to work those areas. On the second day, while on proactive patrol, they monitored a radio call of a burglary in progress around the corner from where they had stationed themselves, in the area they had targeted. They subsequently made an arrest and the burglaries stopped.

- A patrol officer received a narcotics alert bulletin that mapped the location of drug hot spots (see Fig. 6.3). During his routine patrol he made specific attempts to travel through the indicated hot spot area on his beat, observed a narcotics transaction, and subsequently made an arrest of both buyer and seller. This is a rare accomplishment for a uniformed patrol officer in a marked police car.
- District 25 used MAPADS to deploy its directed patrol missions (one for robbery, one for burglary, one for auto theft) every 2 weeks. Maps were provided showing the specific activity and the highest activity areas. Rarely were the same areas high in the same criminal activity for two such periods in a row. It is not known whether this is merely a statistical artifact or whether the maps have made an impact.[2]
- In addition to these specific incidents, the district commander produced map-based crime awareness bulletins (see Figs. 6.4 and 6.5), which often became the basis for crime analysis patterns generated by the CAU (see Fig. 6.6).

One of the most important ramifications of MAPADS was first made evident by a potential pattern that did not materialize. The most prominent characteristic of Figure 6.7 is the narcotics hot spot that was reported by community residents to District 25. The residents had described to the police the extent of drug-selling activity on a stretch of Lemoyne Avenue. When it was plotted on the map that contained other offenses on Beat 2523, it was noticed that there was a concentration of burglaries. primarily commercial burglaries, on nearby streets. This suggested the possibility of a relationship-perhaps people coming into the neighborhood to buy drugs first stopped on North Avenue (a commercial strip) to steal something to pay for the drug transaction.

This possible connection was investigated, but no evidence was found to tie the two activities together. What this example does point out, however, is the substantial benefit of (a) incorporating community information and (b) going beyond just including known offenses on the maps. By incorporating community information. the

---

[2]The specific statistical artifact in question is *regression to the mean*. If there is a great deal of random variation in a quantity (such as the number of car thefts per 2-week period in a beat), then if a beat has a much higher than average number in one period, during the next 2-week period one would expect the number to be lower. This is because if it is very unlikely for the beat to have such a high number in one period, it is doubly unlikely for the beat to be so high twice in a row.

police have the opportunity to see how criminal activity may be affected by other activity of concern to the community. In this case, of course, the activity reported by the community is also criminal, but one can easily extrapolate beyond the data at hand and see the benefit of, say, including on the maps calls regarding disturbances, loud parties, abandoned cars, youths loitering, and so on, and seeing if there is any relationship between these noncriminal community concerns and crime.

Furthermore, those familiar with large municipal departments know what normally happens when burglary and narcotics calls come in. In Chicago, follow-up investigations of burglaries are handled by detectives from the property crimes unit. Follow-up investigations of narcotics calls are handled by the district tactical unit. Similar specialization and division of responsibility take place in other police departments. The two units do not ordinarily compare notes about what may be occurring in the same neighborhood, so even if there is a relationship between the two activity patterns it may not be uncovered. Although the juxtaposition of these two patterns was merely coincidental in this case, it would never have surfaced at all had not the information been mapped.[3] The tactical unit would have investigated only the drug-related activity and the property crime detectives would have tried to infer patterns from the burglary data alone.

Thus, the maps are perceived by district command personnel to have had a direct and tangible impact on policing and crime prevention and analysis in District 25. The researchers and police personnel cooperating in this project were surprised by the extent of adoption and persistent use of the system and feel that it has proved to be an effective tool for patrol use. In addition, use of the 24-hour activity report data in the computer provided District 25 with more usable data than in any other district.

Maps, Patrol, and Memory

It is a naive assumption that merely providing good intelligence to patrol officers would result in their using it effectively. Some beat officers seem to consider the maps both superfluous and a waste of time . We had expected this reaction, especially from the more senior patrol officers; however, many younger officers were cynical as well, and criticized MAPADS during roll call. The younger officers may have been influenced by the older officers to behave in this way, so as not to seem to be too eager about doing their job. The following conversation exemplifies the feeling that MAPADS is a waste of time:[4]

---

[3] It was subsequently found that this type of pattern was replicated in another area-see again Fig. 3.3.

[4] These and subsequent quotes are taken from transcripts of interviews with police officers.

Interviewer: What do you think of the computer mapping project? Are you able to make use of the maps?

Officer: Realistically, do you want me to tell you what you want to hear?

Interviewer: No, the truth.

Officer: The policemen in the street don't give a shit. Management does.

According to other officers, however, the maps are a welcome tool that could be improved:

Officer: How many officers give a shit? Maybe 2 out of 10. Those who don't give a shit will corrupt others. I read them [the maps] regularly. For auto thefts, they're great to see where the slobs are from, bill I also want to know where the cars are recovered from.[5] A map would be much better for this than a narrative.

Many patrol officers feel that they know the geography of their beats pretty well and have no need to be reminded of where incidents take place. In part, this may be their feeling because they interpret the maps' utility too narrowly and need more instruction as to what the maps may convey. This was pointed out by one of the officers who used and supported MAPADS:

Officer: What we need is to have more made of the maps at roll call. Take 10 to 15 minutes at the end to have the watch commander walk through the mapping material with the officers.

Although the maps seem to have been less than enthusiastically welcomed by most patrol officers, there are several reasons for hope. First, a handful of officers in District 25 have made effective use of MAPADS and are enthusiastically supportive of it. Second, there is some evidence that MAPADS use is being underreported and dissatisfaction amplified. This situation results from a desire to avoid paperwork and the opposition of the vocal and perhaps more senior officers. Third, tactical units demonstrate a considerably higher degree of use and appreciation of the maps. Fourth, even the disaffected officers, when queried more specifically, could identify some productive applications. In fact, some suggested improvements were generated by officers who criticized MAPADS, as in the following interchange:

Interviewer: So what use are you able to make of these materials from the computer project?

Officer: It's bullshit. This stuff is totally useless. Statistics aren't any help to patrol officers.

Interviewer: What about the maps?
Officer: We haven't seen much of the maps. From what I have seen, they don't seem to be much good. either. Showing where autos are stolen from is useless. I'd like to know where they're being recovered from. Where they are stripped is going to be close to where the thieves live. Mapping robberies is also useless. Murders, too. And it's not that policemen can't understand it [the maps]; police have become more and more literate.

Interviewer: How about burglaries?

[5]This information was subsequently added to the maps.

Officer: Yeah, burglaries maybe. Young burglars, they usually work their own neighborhoods. Older burglars know better. generally. Sometimes they get greedy. Also. they give us a map just for our own beat. That's stupid. because on any given day you can be on any beat.

Interviewer: You mean you aren't usually on [this beat]?

Officer: This is the first time I've been on it.

In fact. the maps serve as more than a mere reminder of the geography of the incidents: *They serve as the beat's institutional memory.* The official institutional memory, the beat book, is kept in the beat car and contains general material relevant to patrol duties, as well as special attention bulletins, which instruct beat officers to pay particular attention to a specific location, and a beat information sheet. used to describe such matters as schools, places of public amusement, potential trouble spots. and parks found within the beat. It does not contain routine information about recent crime activity on the beat or about other activity of relevance to policing.

The concept of the map as an institutional memory deserves more attention because of the importance and possibilities it brings to policing. The realization of this concept can promote patrol-oriented crime analysis, leading to more effective, community-oriented policing.

One stereotypical image of the patrol officer is that of the friendly cop on the beat, the individual who knows better than anyone else what's going on in the community, who the troublemakers are, and how to handle most community disturbances short of a riot. That is, we conceive of patrol officers as having an instinctive ability to analyze criminal and subcriminal situations and to act appropriately in such situations. But for the most part patrol operations are driven by calls for service, leaving patrol officers with relatively little time to patrol or otherwise explore potential trouble spots in their beats. This in itself does not mean that patrol officers cannot know their beats; after all, presumably the aggregation of all calls for service can be analyzed to pinpoint the trouble spots. But there are other forces that prevent this from occurring.

First, patrol officers do not know everything about what happens on their beat. There are 21 tours of duty in a week, only about 5 of which are covered by any one officer. [Chicago police officers work 6 days on, 2 days off. With vacations and holidays, the average number of tours per week worked by an officer is between 4 and 5.] An officer reporting in at roll call will ordinarily not know what transpired even on the previous shift unless something unusual occurred. Unfortunately, robbery, burglary, and auto theft are not unusual occurrences in large urban areas.

Second, patrol officers do not even know about everything occurring on their beats while they are on patrol. Calls for service are not uniformly distributed over space and time. As a result, when more than one call for service comes in from a single beat, a patrol officer from another beat or even another sector (which is comprised of three or four beats) may be dispatched to handle it. All of this cross-beat and cross-sector dispatching means that perhaps one half of the incidents occurring in a beat are handled by officers from different beats-and perhaps half of the incidents handled by a beat officer are for out-of-beat calls. Thus, their "net beat service" may be the equivalent of only about two shifts per week, or about 10% of the total activity.

Third, not all police officers are interested in what happens on their beats. There are those who have been made cynical by the job and are not invested in it nor interested in making themselves more productive. They put in their time, making sure that they don't do too much work or get in trouble for doing too little. They are what might be called "radio-active" officers-when they receive a call on the radio they handle it (not too quickly, mind you), but when they complete the call they sink back into inactivity. These officers are not likely to be interested in the proactive analysis of criminal (or any other) activity on their beats. In addition, crime analysis per se is not part of the patrol officer's job description. They consider crime analysis to be the domain of detectives and tactical officers.

Fourth, most police departments consider patrol activity to be concerned with incident-oriented policing-that is, they look at each individual incident without considering whether it had any connection to other incidents. Crime analysis as an adjunct of patrol, therefore, has not been a primary concern of police administrators. More recently, however, attention has been focused on problem-oriented policing and on addresses that generate repeated complaints (Goldstein, 1979; Eck & Spelman, 1985).

A fifth reason for the lack of an analysis capability for patrol purposes is the fact that certain community interests have not, for the most part, been of primary concern to police administrators. That is not to say that protecting the community from concern is not the priority of police administrators. Rather, many police officials may have felt that the community is more concerned with incivilities (Hunter, 1978) than with real crime; in meetings with community residents, the police are often more likely to be greeted with complaints about men urinating in the street, teenagers gathering on street corners, and cars abandoned in front of houses than they are about robbery and burglary. In other words, there is a difference in perception between the police and community. For the most part, police are driven by goals related to index crimes rather than by goals more closely related to community concerns about incivilities. Because index crimes are followed up and analyzed by detectives, there is no reason for any analytic capability for patrol officers.

The final reason for the lack of any crime analysis capability in the patrol divisions of most police departments is the sheer numbers involved. A police district in the city of Chicago is the size of a small city; District 25, our pilot district, has a population of about 167,000. Although it may have only about 1,200 index crimes per month, it receives upwards of 9,500 calls for service a month. Detectives, who do crime analysis for police departments, can handle the current volume of index crime; they read through the cases and look for patterns. But they cannot handle eight times the current volume, even if only to sift through the calls.

We have described earlier how maps can serve as a geographically based institutional memory. They can also be the vehicle whereby an effective analytic capability can be added to patrol operations in a police district. This capability need not be confined solely to a crime analysis officer, who is a review officer assigned to concentrate on using MAPADS to analyze crime activity in the district as part of the crime mapping project (see Appendix D), as has been the case in District 25. Nor need it be restricted to use only for repeat complaint addresses and well-defined problems. With every beat officer provided with maps, the potential for beat-by-beat analysis by patrol officers can become a reality.

Summary

Even though we are pleased with the way the maps were used in District 25, they were not as effective as they might have been, for a number of reasons. The crime mapping project walked a fine line between research and operations, and sometimes the two interfered with each other. This is especially true in two areas–training of the officers and documentation of the results. We were interested in getting the maps into use by patrol officers as quickly as possible and therefore did not pave the way by first introducing them and explaining how they might be used in training sessions, then following these sessions up with debriefings, and then developing forms for the officers to fill out for evaluating their utility.

We took a calculated risk by initially providing the maps to patrol officers with only a brief introduction. We wanted to see how they would use them without direction because, quite frankly, we were not sure as to how they might be used and did not want to stifle creative uses that we did not predict. Of course, we did not realize (but should have) that many of the officers would look upon MAPADS as an imposition, not an aid. In hindsight, it was our mistake; these officers were reacting normally to an innovation being thrust upon them without any preparation or training.

We did not want to increase the already heavy report-writing burden on patrol officers by developing forms for them to fill out about how (or whether) they used the maps. This was especially true at the beginning of the project, when we were not sure that the maps would have any beneficial effect on their operations. Our interviews did provide us with insights with respect to the use of the maps, as described in the previous section, but documentation of their use is not as complete as it might have been. This again was a judgment call on our part. After considering the limited resources at our disposal, we decided to direct our primary attention to the development and operationalization of the MAPADS system (including a rather heavy resource commitment to icon placement) and to technical and operational support of the units using it rather than to formal documentation and evaluation of the system.

CHICAGO POLICE DEPARTMENT
25th District
CRIME AWARENESS BULLETIN®

Fred Rice, Superintendent of Police   Matthias E. Casey, District Commander
Volume 1, #6   16 Sep 1987
****

TO: All Members, 025

FROM: District Review Office, Analysis Section

PERSONNEL ARE TO PAY PARTICULAR ATTENTION TO:

North Avenue from 5000 West to 6000 West, and
Division & Laramie, 3rd watch predominately

FOR:

Strong Arm Robberies (Smash & Grab)

Offender is described as M/B 19/25 YOA 160 Black Hair,
Brown Eyes, Dark Complexion. Wearing a combination of
Blue Cord Jacket, Red T-shirt or Navy Blue T-shirt w/writing,
Blue Jeans, Blue or Black Baseball Cap and Gym Shoes. Offender
approaches victim's car and breaks passenger's side window,
taking purse/property.

Related RD#s: J 355 054, J 368 846, J 372 373, J 379 559,
J 379 648, J 389 360, J 391 839, J 393 828

THE DISTRICT COMMANDER SHOULD BE MADE AWARE OF ANY ARRESTS
EFFECTED THROUGH INFORMATION PROVIDED BY THIS BULLETIN

Thank you,

CONFIDENTIAL - FOR POLICE USE ONLY

Figure 6.1 Crime awareness bulletin regarding
strong-arm robberies in District 25.

25th DISTRICT

CHICAGO POLICE DEPARTMENT
CONFIDENTIAL - For Police Use Only

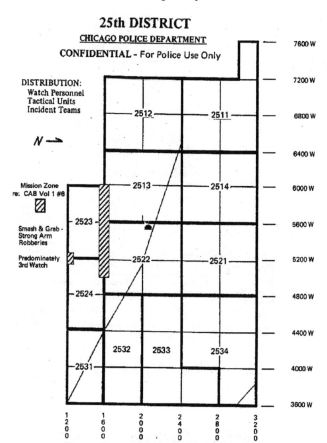

DISTRIBUTION:
Watch Personnel
Tactical Units
Incident Teams

Mission Zone
re: CAB Vol 1 #6

Smash & Grab -
Strong Arm
Robberies

Predominately
3rd Watch

Figure 6.1. continued

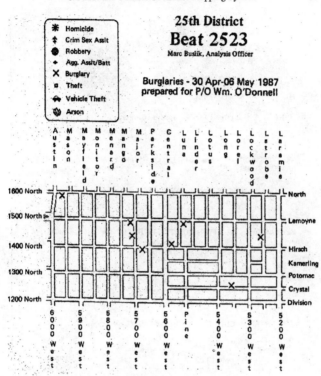

Figure 6.2. Computer-generated map showing
locations of daytime burglaries

CHICAGO POLICE DEPARTMENT
25th District

NARCOTICS ALERT BULLETIN®

Matthias E. Casey, District Commander   Marc Buslik, Analysis Officer
Volume 1, #1   28 Oct 1987

TO: All Members, 025

FROM: District Review Office, Analysis Section

ANALYSIS INDICATES THAT THE FOLLOWING BEAT(S) HAVE THE HIGHEST
NARCOTICS RELATED ACTIVITY

Beats 2523, 2531 and 2532

PAY PARTICULAR ATTENTION TO THE FOLLOWING HOT SPOT(S):

Vicinity of Lockwood and Potomac,
Lockwood and Lemoyne
Vicinity of Pulaski and Division,
Harding and Division
Vicinity of Lemoyne and Lawndale

CURRENT STREET VALUES (per gram):

Marijuana	$ 2.77	Cocain	$ 142.00
(Hawaiian	14.11)	Heroin-Brown	77.72
Thai Sticks	@ 10.00	White	129.60
LSD	140.00	PCP	96.00

THE DISTRICT COMMANDER SHOULD BE MADE AWARE OF ANY ARRESTS
EFFECTED THROUGH INFORMATION PROVIDED BY THIS BULLETIN

Thank you,

CONFIDENTIAL - FOR POLICE USE ONLY

Figure 6.3. A narcotics alert bulletin that
led to arrests in a drug hot spot

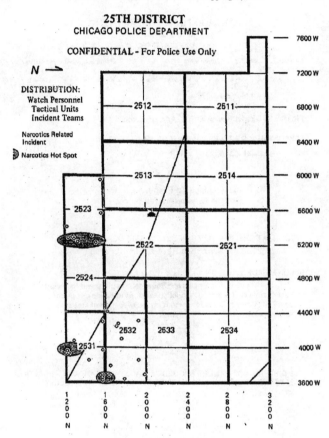

Figure 6.3. continued

CHICAGO POLICE DEPARTMENT
25th District

CRIME AWARENESS BULLETIN ®

Matthias E. Casey, District Commander   Marc Busiik, Analysis Officer
Volume 2, #12   11 Aug 88

* *

TO: All Members, 025

FROM: District Review Office, Analysis Section

PERSONNEL ARE TO PAY PARTICULAR ATTENTION TO:
           Beat 2514, 3rd Watch

FOR:

           Criminal Damage To Property;
           Broken windows in residences

SPECIAL ATTENTION TO THE FOLLOWING LOCATION(s):
           2958 N. Major; See Reverse Side for Map

RECOMMENDED ACTION

           Beat cars. Sector cars and Squadrols should spend increased
free patrol time in this area. Conduct street stops of suspicious persons.
Prepare Field Contact Cards for persons interviewed. **Street stops**
prevent these offenses!

THE DISTRICT COMMANDER SHOULD BE MADE AWARE OF ANY ARRESTS
EFFECTED THROUGH INFORMATION PROVIDED BY THIS BULLETIN

                   Thank you,

                   Capt. John Rogers

CONFIDENTIAL - FOR POLICE USE ONLY

Figure 6.6. Example of a crime awareness bulletin
that became the basis for a crime analysis pattern

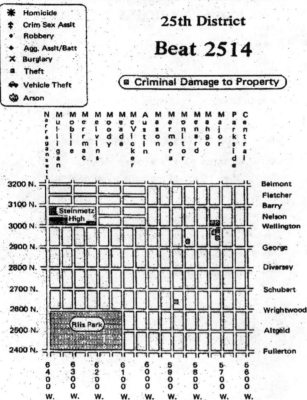

CHICAGO POLICE DEPARTMENT

25th District

Beat 2514

Figure 6.4. continued

CHICAGO POLICE DEPARTMENT
25th District

CRIME AWARENESS BULLETIN ©

Matthias E. Casey, District Commander   Marc Buslik, Analysis Officer
Volume 2, #14   19 Oct 88

****

TO: All Members, 025

FROM: District Review Office, Analysis Section

PERSONNEL ARE TO PAY PARTICULAR ATTENTION TO:

BEAT 2521

FOR.   **Residential Garage Burglaries**

SPECIAL ATTENTION TO THE FOLLOWING LOCATION

(See attached map for locations)

RECOMMENDED ACTION

     Beat cars, Sector cars and Squadrols should spend increased free patrol time in this area. Watch for suspicious persons loitering around area. Patrol alleys and watch for persons with snowblowers, lawnmowers and bicycles, walking down and coming out of alleys. Prepare field contact cards for persons interviewed. Remember - field interviews prevent these offenses.

THE DISTRICT COMMANDER SHOULD BE MADE AWARE OF ANY ARRESTS
EFFECTED THROUGH INFORMATION PROVIDED BY THIS BULLETIN

Thank you,

M E Casey

CONFIDENTIAL - FOR POLICE USE ONLY

Figure 6.5. Example of a crime awareness bulletin
that became the basis for a crime analysis pattern

CHICAGO POLICE DEPARTMENT

25th District
Beat 2521
Garage Burglaries
16 Sep - 17 Oct 1988

Figure 6.5. continued

88.09.16 2300 / 0800	Burglary Forcible Entry	48 Allgeld 2521 K 405014	Entry was made thru rear door of garage. Loss at this time. Misc. tools.
88.09.17 0500 / 0600	Buglary Forcible Entry	50--Montrose K 402579	Garage door. 1 B/S D Cordless grass shears Model # 8288 1 Sears Gas lawnmower A65338D300 & much more
88.09.28 0100 / 1100	Burglary Forcible Entry	F2 - Wolfram K 424783	Entry was made thru side door of garage. Loss at this time. Lawnmower.
88/09/23 0100 / 0100	Burglary Forcible Entry	48--Berry K 425142	Entry was made thru side door of garage. Loss at this time. Misc. tools.
 2100 / 0700	Burglary Forcible Entry	52 Oakdale K 425091	Entry was made thru side door of garage. Loss at this time. Auto Radio.
88/09/29 0700 / 1000	Burglary Forcible Entry	F0--Wolfram K 425780	Garage door. One Skill saw, One screwdriver and one Chop saw. No makes or serial numbers listed.
88/10/00 1430	Burglary Forcible Entry	49--Damen K 430111	Entry was made thru side door of garage. Loss at this time. Misc. tools.
 2100 / 2300	Burglary Forcible Entry	46---Argeld K 434093	Entry was made thru side door of garage. Loss at this time. Bikes.
88/10/05 1900 / 7200	Burglary Forcible Entry	51--Wolfram K 438403	Entry was made thru side door of garage. Loss at this time. Snowblower.
88/10/09 0900 / 1200	Burglary Forcible Entry	51--Washington K 440054	Garage door. Offender(s) took a brand new tune up analysis kit. Brand new still in box. Make & model unk.
88/10/11 0100 / 1430	Burglary Forcible Entry	50--Sawyer K 443389	Garage door. Offender(s) took Lawnmower and miscellaneous hand tools & damaged tools on car
 0730 / 0930	Burglary Forcible Entry	49 - Drummond K 448516	Garage door. Offender(s) took socket sets and other miscellaneous tools and tool trays
 0745 / 0900	Burglary Forcible Entry	49--Drummond K 448396	Garage door. Four items and tires taken. No make or description or tire #'s given.
88/10/13 1700 / 0000	Burglary Forcible Entry	50 Wolfram 2521 K 451533	Entry was made thru side door of garage. Loss at this time. Lawnmower.
88/10/14 0000 / 1900	Burglary Forcible Entry	53--Wolfram K 454375	Entry was made thru side door of garage. Loss at this time. Bike.
88/10/16 1800 / 1000	Burglary Forcible Entry	53--Berry K 454996	Entry was made thru side door of garage. Loss at this time. Misc. tools.
 2200 / 0800	Burglary Forcible Entry	53--Oakdale K 456777	Garage door. Taken 1 Gas snow thrower, 1 Air Compressor. 1 Portable Air compressor. Makes not listed.
88/10/17 0000 / 1700	Burglary Forcible Entry	48--Damen K 456311	Entry was made thru side door of garage. Loss at this time. Misc. tools.

Figure 6.5. continued

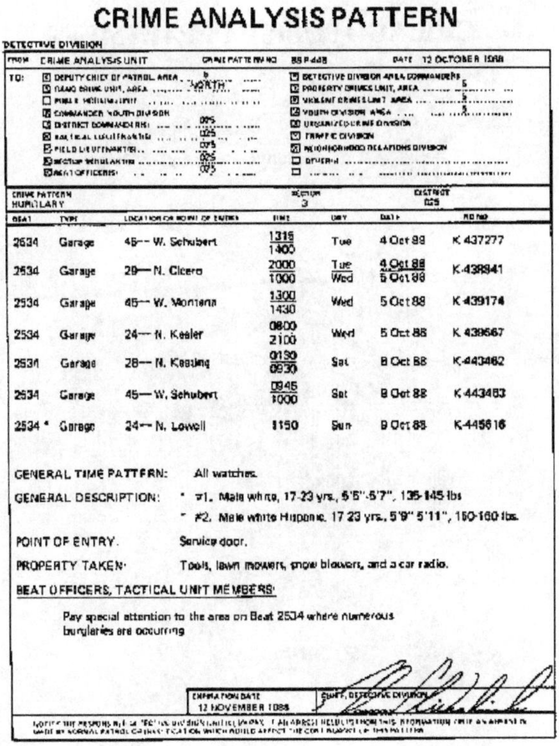

CRIME ANALYSIS PATTERN

DETECTIVE DIVISION

FROM: CRIME ANALYSIS UNIT — CRIME PATTERN NO. 88 P 448 — DATE 12 OCTOBER 1988

TO: DEPUTY CHIEF OF PATROL, AREA NORTH; COMMANDER YOUTH DIVISION; DISTRICT COMMANDER(S) 025; FIELD LIEUTENANT(S) 025; BEAT OFFICERS 025; DETECTIVE DIVISION AREA COMMANDER(S); PROPERTY CRIMES UNIT, AREA 5; VIOLENT CRIMES UNIT AREA 5; YOUTH DIVISION AREA 5; TRAFFIC DIVISION; NEIGHBORHOOD RELATIONS DIVISION; OTHER(S)

CRIME PATTERN: BURGLARY — SECTOR: 3 — DISTRICT: 025

BEAT	TYPE	LOCATION OR POINT OF ENTRY	TIME	DAY	DATE	RD NO
2534	Garage	45-- W. Schubert	1315 / 1400	Tue	4 Oct 88	K 437277
2534	Garage	29— N. Cicero	2000 / 1000	Tue / Wed	4 Oct 88 / 5 Oct 88	K 438841
2534	Garage	46— W. Montana	1300 / 1430	Wed	5 Oct 88	K 439174
2534	Garage	24— N. Kesler	0800 / 2100	Wed	5 Oct 88	K 439567
2534	Garage	28— N. Keating	0130 / 0930	Sat	8 Oct 88	K 443462
2534	Garage	45— W. Schubert	0945 / 1000	Sat	8 Oct 88	K 443463
2534 *	Garage	24— N. Lowell	1150	Sun	9 Oct 88	K 445616

GENERAL TIME PATTERN: All watches.

GENERAL DESCRIPTION: * #1. Male white, 17-23 yrs., 5'5"-5'7", 135-145 lbs
* #2. Male white Hispanic, 17-23 yrs., 5'9"-5'11", 150-160 lbs.

POINT OF ENTRY: Service door.

PROPERTY TAKEN: Tools, lawn mowers, snow blowers, and a car radio.

BEAT OFFICERS, TACTICAL UNIT MEMBERS:

Pay special attention to the area on Beat 2534 where numerous burglaries are occurring

EXPIRATION DATE: 12 NOVEMBER 1988 — CHIEF, DETECTIVE DIVISION

Figure 6.6. Example of crime analysis pattern made possible by use of MAPADS.

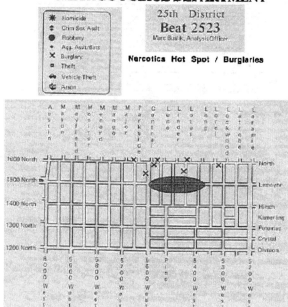

Figure 6.7. MAPADS-generated map showing
narcotics hot spot.

CHAPTER 7

Detective Use of the Mapping System

MAPADS was implemented in the Area 5 violent crimes unit on a pilot basis. It was used only for robbery cases for a period of 5 months (January-June, 1988). Although the system proved to be effective even in this limited implementation, its effectiveness depended greatly on how information was entered and maintained in MAPADS and on the reward structure (both real and perceived) with respect to information sharing by detectives. In this chapter we describe (a) how the volume of crimes relates to detective specialization, (b) issues relating to the sharing of information by detectives, (c) how MAPADS was used during the implementation, and (d) the data entry problems experienced in this implementation.

Specialization by Detectives

As discussed in Chapter 1, police departments collect so much information that it becomes difficult to process it all effectively. Therefore, police departments divide up the work load; with respect to patrol, the division is geographic, forming districts, sectors, and beats; with respect to detective work, the division is first geographic (by area) and then by type of case so that each detective knows a great deal about some types of cases in his or her Area. There are six areas in the city of Chicago, each comprising between 3 and 5 of the 25 districts and about one-half million residents. Each detective area has a violent crimes unit and a property crimes unit. Each detective specializes in one type of crime: burglary, robbery, sex crimes, or homicide. This has the advantage that each detective learns all about one type of crime. Speaking of his days in the field, one detective interviewed in the crime mapping project pointed out the advantages of specialization:

As a detective in burglary, burglary was burglary. If you ran into something [else] you took care of it, but mostly you did burglary. You knew them. They came out with a list, all the known burglars–every car they had, their name, address, who their friends were. You would look for burglars. When you saw one, you stop and talk to them. Bring them in, take a new photo. The burglary dicks knew the burglars. Robbery knew robbers. Homicide-those just happen. Cartage thieves, knew 'em.

Specialization by detectives is predicated on the assumption that offenders generally specialize by type of crime themselves so that, for example, detectives looking for a burglar would not need to keep track of sex crimes to collect information that might be useful. This specialization is justified by the detectives' experience (see Sanders, 1977). Because detectives cannot analyze all of the crime information that is generated by the area, focusing their attention on specific types of crime allows them to increase their chances of finding relevant information. The advantage of this specialization is that each detective learns a great deal about one type of crime and thus about one class of offenders.

There are some notable exceptions, however, to the benefits of specialization. Certain classes of crimes overlap regularly. For example, some crimes that start out as sex crimes turn into robberies (and vice versa) if the assailant is either unsuccessful or interrupted. Burglaries that find the owner home can turn into robbery, assault, or even homicide. A purse snatching is sometimes classified as larceny, sometimes as robbery, depending on the extent of force used to steal the purse. In addition, one detective suggested that criminals today are not specializing as much as they once did; that is, there are fewer professional burglars or professional robbers.

Accounting for these cross-classifications is not difficult if the detective is able to determine the initial motivation of the offender. Other types of cross- classifications are not as easy to track, as the following indicates:

I had these intimidations. The guy was arrested for battery. But I didn't know it. I get an intimidations case report in my box. I call the victim. She's got a complaint against him for battery and now he's making phone calls. She doesn't know him, but he's been bothering her. Every time he calls she makes out a report. There are four reports with four different detectives. There's even a warrant for the guy, but I don't know it. Finally he's brought in on the warrant and someone says to me, "Hey, don't you have a similar case?"

Fragmentation and Sharing of Information

In 1980, in an attempt to deal with the fragmentation of knowledge that results from specialization, the CPD reorganized detectives into two broad specialties and assigned them to one of two units, property crimes or violent crimes. Property crimes detectives handle all cases dealing with burglary, theft, fraud, and other property crimes. Violent crimes detectives deal with robbery, sex crimes, homicide, assault, and other violent crimes. Thus, detectives are supposed to be generalists within these two areas. However, specialists have reemerged within both units, as the following quote indicates:

They're going back to specialization. When they made the change in 1980. a few months after they made the change they knew it was a mistake .... Now we [violent crimes] have robbery and sex specialists, and they've just added homicide.

In addition to the difficulty that the Department encounters with crimes that cross specialties, the current organization suffers from a fragmentation problem for the high-volume crimes of burglary and robbery. This is caused by the conflicting need to maintain specialization while equalizing work loads. An area may average about 60 burglaries and 15 robberies a day. Because of the volume of these crimes, not just the robbery or burglary specialists investigate those crimes; all property crimes detectives get some burglaries and all violent crimes detectives get some robberies. Although this helps even out the work load, it also means that no one in the area investigates all the robberies or all the burglaries. This leads to a fragmentation of information because similar cases can go to different detectives.

There are two places in the detective division where all cases get reviewed, the case management sergeant (CMS) in the Area and the CAU downtown. The CMS is supposed to read every case and assign cases that need follow-up investigation to the appropriate detectives. His or her ability to remember similar cases and assign them to the same detective is one mechanism for overcoming this fragmentation problem. (Of course, this mechanism is less effective when the CMS takes days off or gets a different assignment.) Second, the CAU detectives read all of the cases in their specialty to try to discover patterns, which they then pass on to the field units. Both the CMS and the CAU serve as means of counteracting fragmentation.

If volume were lower, the combination of the CMS, the headquarters CAU reviewing the cases, and the detectives themselves would likely overcome much of this problem. However, the volume of crimes is high enough to stretch the limits of memory. Thus, the detectives need some mechanism for storing and retrieving the information contained in the case files so that they can access that information, first for all the similar cases and second, for those cases that occasionally become related due to the special circumstances noted above. This is particularly important for combinations that cross the violent crimes-property crimes separation, such as a purse snatching that becomes a robbery or a burglary that becomes an assault.

Detectives have implemented several solutions to this problem of sharing information. First, they develop paper files. Second, they use computer files. Third, they share information face to face, either formally or informally. Each of these solutions has some advantages and some inherent difficulties. The problems with each of these solutions reflect the nature of the organization within which the solutions are embedded.

Paper Files

The most common solution to sharing information is in the paper files kept by the area. As discussed earlier, the area receives a photocopy of all case reports on crimes within the Area's borders. Additional photocopies (more paper!) are then made for other files kept by the area. They include a chronological file; an MO file; and, for high-volume crimes, additional files for crime subcategories.

The chronological file is a listing of all cases, filed by case number (which is generally chronological). This permits detectives to look up cases if they have the case numbers, This file is complete and contains all of the information needed for any of these integrative purposes, but it is not very useful when trying to tie cases together because searches can only be made by date or case number.

Each section has its own MO file. This file lists all recent suspended cases by type of crime. This file is useful in that it allows detectives to look for similar cases. However, because the file is only referenced by incident-and then only by primary incident. district and date-there is no simple way to look for the characteristic similarities in which detectives are interested, such as unusual descriptions or methods. The only way to obtain such information is to leaf through all of the case reports individually.

To alleviate this situation somewhat, the high-volume crimes are further subdivided. For example, robbery is divided by type of location (factory, restaurant, small store, bank, etc.), with a separate file for street robberies. Street robberies are further subdivided by race and number of offenders, with special folders for unknown offenders (hit from behind) and female offenders (there are so few female offenders that all are patternable). There are also clipboards with all active cases. For example, in the violent crimes unit there are clipboards for robbery by district, sexual assault, miscellaneous sex offenses, and unlawful use of weapons, with additional clipboards for administrative purposes and law enforcement agencies data system (LEADS) messages from throughout the city and suburbs.

These files and clipboards are useful sources of information for detectives and help alleviate the fragmentation problem. Detectives review the boards daily to look for recent similar cases in order to discover patterns and solve cases. However, these searches are cumbersome. The robbery board for an active district might have several hundred cases, covering a 3-month period.

In addition to the standard files, files have been developed for special purposes. Area detectives who have used them (e.g., to track career criminals) feel that paper systems are too cumbersome. This becomes especially apparent when it becomes necessary to analyze criminal career records not just by name but by different characteristics; paper files don't readily lend themselves to cross-referencing.

Because of the high volume of robbery cases, particularly over time (as is the case for a career criminal file), paper files become quickly unusable. This is particularly true because detectives want to be able to search for unique characteristics A cases or offenders, which are hard to build into a paper file referencing system. The high volume of data and the limits of the paper system lead to information overload. There is so much information that most of it becomes virtually useless. Because of the limitations of paper files, the detectives who took part in the crime .napping project were enthusiastic about MAPADS's ability to search through the narrative and offender characteristics fields and retrieve similar cases. thereby -educing some of the information fragmentation and overload problems.

Computer Files

Detectives may also use RAMIS to review all cases with certain characteristics. An additional advantage of using RAMIS is that it eliminates another aspect of the fragmentation problem, the separation of the city into six areas. However, once they have conducted a RAMIS search using the data fields that are keyed into the computer, detectives must then find the paper copies of the reports and read the narratives to find out if the cases are similar. If the other incidents are in their area, they can find them easily; if the incidents are in other areas, the detectives would normally travel to the other areas to pick up copies of the reports (and any supplemental reports as well), or request that a copy be sent from the other area or from the records division.

Personal Contacts

An alternative strategy for overcoming information fragmentation is the use of personal contacts. Detectives will occasionally pass information to each other in order to fill in gaps in their knowledge. Such interaction allows for the sharing of information (because no field detective can read all of the case reports). But this implies that those detectives with information relevant to another detective's case *know* that it is relevant to the case; otherwise, it is a hit-or-miss proposition as to whether the information gets communicated. Furthermore, the use of personal contacts is constrained by several organizational factors that limit the amount of interaction among detectives.

There is little time available for the routinized sharing of information among detectives. They may arrive at work a few minutes before their shift to get ready for the roll call. Then they spend most of their time out of the office, answering calls or conducting interviews. The roll call is supposed to be an opportunity for the police to share their information. However, it is rare to see detectives sharing information about cases at roll call. Some say that they occasionally share information at roll call, but others say that very little information is shared then. This suggests that roll call is one time when information *can* be shared. Furthermore, there is no formalized means for detectives to share this information, as the following dialogue suggests:

Interviewer: So you only share this information over coffee?

Detective 1: Right. Other than that, there's no formal meeting

Detective 2: We have roll call, but there's not much exchange of information. Everyone is in a different direction on a handout. No one else knows what you are doing.

Many detectives occasionally talk about their cases with other detectives over coffee or in the halls. They also often "talk shop" when socializing. Skolnick (1967) provides a discussion of the high degree of intergroup socializing among police officers. However, this information sharing is of limited utility because of another organizational constraint, that is, the perceptions held by detectives of how they are evaluated.

Impediments to Information Sharing

Detectives are evaluated on a regular basis. There is a strong feeling among the detectives interviewed for the crime mapping project that this evaluation, particularly for the field detectives, is in large part based on the number of arrests they make. Arrests formally make up only a small percentage of the total evaluation. Command personnel from the detective division told us that no one had been demoted because of low arrest productivity since 1979. However, the area detectives interviewed felt strongly that they were being pressured to produce arrests. These are in fact not inconsistent observations. Whereas the evaluation may be made up of numerous factors, arrests might be the marginal factor that distinguishes good candidates from fair ones. In addition, although not making arrests may not be sufficient ground for demotion, it may be sufficient to prevent promotion or selection for choice assignments. Because detectives are out in the field, and because there is no "cookbook" on how to solve particular cases, they are pretty much on their own. They can do what they want, as long as they are reasonably productive, and as long as they concentrate on major crimes as they come up.

This autonomy is one characteristic of professionals (Freidson, 1970; Hughes, 1984). Detectives feel that their work, like that of doctors and lawyers, involves a lot of on-the-spot judgment. Their work is not easily routinized into a set of rules delineating what they should be doing every moment of the day. Like the law firm's emphasis on billable hours, the emphasis on arrests is one way of supervising professionals through output. In addition, supervisors want to be perceived as fair in order to prevent criticism from their staff and to prevent charges of favoritism or discrimination. An objective measure of performance such as arrests gives them the opportunity to present their evaluations as fair.

Because detectives feel they are evaluated on the number of arrests, some may withhold information from other detectives if that information will lead to an arrest. For example, if a detective knows that an offender always hits cab drivers at a certain time in a certain neighborhood, the detective may withhold that information from colleagues until he or she can get free to sit and wait for the next robbery rather than pass on the information so someone else can arrest the offender sooner.

Although such a strategy is irrational for the *organization*, the *individual* perceives it as rational, and it is a direct result of the organization's need to evaluate on results. Unlike hockey players, detectives are not normally given points for assists. Perhaps this should change if information sharing is to become a reality. Currently, however, detectives will only share information when they are stumped, that is, when they have no hope of making an arrest, but hope that by sharing information they will find the piece missing from the puzzle. Detectives interviewed for the crime mapping project commented that the information received from such interactions was in general of very low quality, because each wanted to give as little as possible and gain as much as possible. This data hoarding was a problem noted in almost all of the interviews.[1] One detective summarized the general sentiment on sharing information as follows:

---

[1]A similar form of data hoarding goes on between police organizations; for example, there are indications that it has been a problem between the FBI and local, state, and even other federal agencies.

There's competition within the department, not personally, but you have to justify your job, why you are a detective and not in uniform. We pass the competency exam, like the exempt. We're not civil service, we can be removed. You can't work for 8 hours and not produce anything. We don't produce cabinets or statues. We have to do our job, which is arresting people, from the case reports. Just handling process jobs is not enough.

We must, based on the case reports. track down or identify the suspect and physically make the arrest. We have an arrest book and all arrests are noted in the book along with the CB number and that's a head. We can't exist without heads.

If you throw out the information you have, we're not all walking around being secretive, but if you're too open, others will find the person and get credit for the arrest. Supposedly, if you work on the case. your name is on the record too, but that's bullshit; only if you identify the person.

If you tell others, you get nothing. It's not 100% written in stone. You will trade information on difficult cases. The easy ones, you do. You generally keep secrecy within you and your partner. If you're standing there with nothing after three months, you better start putting names in that arrest book. If they put new detectives in. they'll send some old ones who aren't producing out.[2]

I agree with this system. It's generally a self-motivated job. This gives you an incentive, if you want to stay you have to produce. I could do nothing all day. I would have to respond to process jobs, but the rest of the time, what I do is my own motivation. But if I don't do enough, soon I'll be back in the district.

This detective felt the current system was reasonable given the nature of detective work. However. others we interviewed felt that a system that gave credit to all those who had worked on a case would encourage cooperation and lead to a more efficient department.

There is also competition between detectives and patrol officers over arrests. particularly between detectives and district tactical (tac) officers, as the following quote indicates:

They steal our arrests. We get a report with a name on it and it's 3 days old. We go out and find out the tac guy made the arrest already.

Tactical officers may pull the carbon of a case report before it is typed onto the 24-hour activity report by the review officer. This gives them time to work on the case before the community is informed about it, which may be necessary in order for them to be successful. But because the detectives may not get a copy of the case report for a few days. it can also serve to undercut the area detectives' effectiveness.

Detectives also spoke of some useful interactions with their colleagues, but these were based on personal ties of trust. Individual detectives stated that there are certain

[2]This is the detective's perception, which is belied by CPD practice. The perception, however, may be reflected more in placing unproductive detectives in unappealing assignments than in actual demotion.

other detectives, patrol officers, and tactical officers whom they trust and who trust them. They share information more freely with these individuals because they know that they would include each other on any arrest made, as the following quote indicates:

Interviewer: Do you work with patrol officers?

Detective 1: If we're looking for someone, we know certain patrol officers. If they're the type we want to give info to, we'll let them know what we want and they'll look in their spare time, while they're cruising. There are certain ones we know, you develop a relationship with them. You know, I work well with X

But even in such circumstances, it was not clear how much credit anyone received for a co-arrest. Thus, the informal information sharing only partially overcomes the fragmentation problem, because information sharing only occurs within a detective's network. As Granovetter (1973) notes, such dependence on networks reduces the value of interaction because the network loses the information possessed by those outside the network, and such outsiders are more likely to have information that would be different from that inside the network.

Exceptions to this rule of data hoarding are the specialist teams (robbery, burglary, sex crimes, homicide, check fraud, and a few others)[3] and the "big cases." In the case of specialties, if a specialist of one type comes across information that is not relevant to his specialty but is relevant to another, he will pass that information along, as indicated in the following example:

Interviewer: Do you work with other detectives on cases?

Detective: Yes. Especially other detectives who handle sex cases. There is a flow of information between us.

Interviewer: Do you have regular meetings?

Detective: No. Mostly at the change of watch, we'll exchange a few words.

Interviewer: How about the other detectives, not the sex detectives?

Detective: Whatever information I have which might be helpful to them I'll give them. In general, if I'm investigating a sex case and during the background check I find out the person has a history of robbery or burglary, I might bring that to the attention of those who handle those types of cases.

[3]Although there are now specialty teams for most types of crimes, most detectives are not specialists. However, as noted above, this is beginning to change. To the extent that the organization emphasizes specialists over generalists, some of the problems of data hoarding may diminish.

Because of the belief that criminals tend to specialize, specialist detectives feel that they lose little by giving out information relevant to other specialties; to the extent that other specialists reciprocate, they gain. In addition, specialists are primarily responsible for their own specialty and so are less likely to follow up on cases outside their specialty. Thus, by giving that information to other detectives, they increase the efficiency of the unit. This suggests that specialty units are a good way to overcome some of the fragmentation problem.

Fragmentation is also a smaller problem on big cases. Although a mission team is assigned exclusively to work those cases, everyone in the unit gets involved. For example, all murders are big cases in the violent crimes unit. The property crimes unit also has its big cases. During the course of the crime mapping project, there was a series of safe burglaries, which the detectives were having a lot of trouble solving and which was making the unit look bad. Everyone in the property crimes unit was assigned to try to solve the case in addition to their regular work load, as discussed in the following interview:

Detective: [The safe burglaries have] been going on about a month. Mostly fast food places. Roof entry, break in, cut holes in the roof, or through a vent or trap door. Drill into the safe.

Interviewer: How many are working on these cases?

Detective: Almost everyone. A group was detailed on it. They're working midnights. The ones who aren't detailed are handling the investigation when they come in. We'll interview the owner or the manager and whoever discovered it. Have the scene processed by the evidence techs. If it's in a residential area, we'll canvass the neighborhood looking for anyone who might have seen something. We make a detailed report. It gets passed up to channels and to the guys at night on the detail.

In these big cases, it is more important that the case be solved than for individuals to get credit, because the whole unit looks bad if they go unsolved. This suggests that perhaps evaluating the unit as a whole rather than evaluating its members individually may help reduce fragmentation.

Thus, personal contacts help overcome information overload by filtering the information and channeling it to the proper detectives. But because the incentive structure encourages data hoarding, personal contacts only partially overcome the fragmentation of information. This, then, is the context in which MAPADS was implemented in the Area 5 violent crimes unit.

MAPADS, Information, and Detectives

The specialization of detectives means that multioffense crimes may be handled by detectives in different units, and the tendency of detectives not to share information means that no one really has an overview of the characteristics of even the same type of crime. With a paper system of reporting, there is no danger of one detective reading another detective's reports to get additional information about a case he or she is trying to put together; there are just too many cases to read through to find anything useful. Putting all of the information about the crime on the computer, however, would mean that the information would be shared by anyone who used the computer system. There was concern that this might affect both the amount and the type of information entered into the computer. This concern did not appear to be warranted, at least for the pilot implementation; this does not mean, however, that it should be ignored in future implementations.

The MAPADS system was never fully integrated into the routines of Area 5 detectives. This was due to the limited computer facilities of the project and the technical limits of the software used. Because an area covers such a large region (one sixth of the city of Chicago), manual entry of all crime data and placement of icons was not feasible, as it was in the district.

However, even with the limited resources devoted to MAPADS in Area 5, a great deal was learned about the analysis needs of detectives. The primary result was the design of a data base that emphasized MO information and descriptions of offenders. By using a free-form text field for an abstract of the narrative information (distilled by detective personnel from the narrative on the original case report), detectives were able to take advantage of the individual identifying information (see Fig. 7.1). This information is on the original case report but is not in the CRIMES data base residing on the mainframe. By entering this information into the microcomputer, Area 5 detectives were able to take advantage of the computer's ability to search through a large number of records. Finally, by combining mapping, fixed data (time, date, offense code, etc.). and free data (narrative), detectives were able to take advantage of the contextual information that MAPADS provided and that their previous data-gathering procedures did not. The analysis of taxicab robberies described below provides an example of how context provides clues that fixed data do not. In this case, the context provided the information that helped overcome a miscoding problem and showed the geographic proximity that allowed the police to set up a stakeout and make an arrest.

Taxicab Robbery Pattern

Although it was not anticipated that any benefits would accrue immediately from the use of MAPADS by Area 5 detectives, this aspect of the project surprised us by bearing fruit within the first 2 weeks of its implementation. As discussed earlier, robberies were mapped by detectives in the Area 5 violent crimes unit on an experimental basis from January to June 1988. We had originally thought that it would take about 1 month before any results might be forthcoming from this effort. That is, we thought that with 1 month's worth of data there would be a sufficiently large data base so that patterns would emerge. It turned out that it took considerably less time for results to appear.

On January 7, 1988, due to the use of the map, Area 5 detectives found a pattern of armed robberies of cab drivers (see Fig. 7.2). All three robberies occurred within a block of each other but may not have been detected by other means because: (a) one of the crimes was coded as a street robbery rather than a taxicab robbery-the detectives picked it up by reading the case narrative-and (b) one of the victims walked into the District station to make the report, thus disguising the location of the incident on the incident report.

The detectives submitted their information to the crime analysis unit, which quickly issued a crime analysis pattern (see Fig. 7.3). Subsequently, on January 11, 1988, two more taxicab robberies were added to the pattern. On January 12, an arrest was made, based on and due to the use of MAPADS. The data display in the mapping system provided a view of the data that raised the suspicions of an experienced detective, who discerned a pattern in spite of the inaccurate data. This is an example of the power steering concept; the computer system alone was misleading, but the detective was able to use his experience and initiative to pursue the clues on the map and find a pattern which he would not have seen without the computer. The area detectives see MAPADS as providing a major improvement in their abilities to detect patterns more rapidly and to respond appropriately. Although they spent a great deal of time entering robbery data into the microcomputer, they still felt that it was worth the effort to do so and regretted the termination of the experiment and the loss of the borrowed computer.

Additional Uses

The flexibility of a decentralized system encouraged the use of MAPADS for particular purposes. For example, a purse snatching in December 1987 resulted in the victim being seriously injured and later dying. The offender was not found, but the offense changed from robbery to homicide. The Area 5 MAPADS unit, which had focused on robberies but not on all purse snatchings (which are sometimes classified as thefts and sometimes as robberies), was asked to support this investigation. It collected all purse snatchings in a seven-beat area surrounding the incident and mapped them, as well as any new incidents occurring in those beats.

The offender was not found, so we are unable to term this application a success. But the fact that the area detectives were able to set up a specialized analysis in MAPADS in a very short time-it took less than 1 day to get a listing of the old cases from the mainframe CRIMES database, pull the old case reports, and set up a regular flow of new case reports from the case management sergeant to the MAPADS team-shows the value of locating such analytic capability in field offices, in order to have the flexibility to respond to short-term, specialized, analysis needs.

Data Entry

We should point out that, by design, data were entered into the MAPADS data base by detectives, not by clerks. This is one area where further research is needed. There was strong disagreement among those interviewed as to whether narrative information should be entered by detectives, by patrol officers or by clerical workers. Some detectives feel that they must enter the data (at least the narrative information) into the system because the narrative has to be interpreted. They did not feel that civilians were capable of the job, and they felt that patrol officers made too many mistakes to be reliable. In fact, one of the duties of detectives is to reclassify cases that have been misclassified by patrol officers (e.g., changing a burglary to a theft or an assault to a robbery). The following exchange indicates two detectives' ideas about data entry:

Interviewer: What about the review officers in the district entering the data?

Detective 1: You need a detective. He has the ability to pick out the points which add to the solvability of the crime. He knows what a detective would need from doing the job. We're not better than the patrol officers; we're experienced.

Detective 2: He's right about detectives. I know what I need, so I know what you want.

Interviewer: If you gave 10 reports to each of 10 detectives, would they all be different?

Detective 2: They'd be similar, but different.

Detective 1: They'd include the high points. The terms would be different. Length different.

Thus, detectives felt that analyzing the narrative from the case report is one of the skills of a detective and that for MAPADS to be useful to detectives the narrative information must be entered by an experienced detective. Several detectives mentioned that an experienced detective assigned to limited duty would be ideal for this job. In contrast, some detectives and command personnel felt that the job should go to clerical workers, because these workers already enter the fixed data from the case report. Although a clerical worker could type in the narrative as written (usually about one paragraph long), narratives occasionally run to several pages.

Therefore, the narrative needs to be distilled before being entered into the computer. Access to the narrative information is one of the most important characteristics of the detective data base and is what primarily distinguishes it from the RAMIS data base. All the interviews with detectives during the crime mapping project indicated that MAPADS would be useful primarily as a means of collecting and analyzing the narrative information. This narrative information, which gives the details of the case, is the key to solving cases for the detective. It was not clear whether or not civilians or even patrol officers would be competent to distill the important information from the narrative. On the other hand, it was clear that detectives did not feel that they should be burdened with the rather major task of entering narrative information from every case.[4] This is one problem with MAPADS that was not worked out during the crime mapping project and will require additional research.

By reading case report narratives, detectives hope to find similarities in description, methods, weapons, and so on, which help them to identify offenders. MAPADS allows detectives to search easily through a large number of narratives by certain relevant characteristics, characteristics that might be different for each search. This contextual information (e.g., "asked for change of a $5 bill," "asked for directions," "spoke Spanish," "wore a green jacket," etc.) is what helps to distinguish cases committed by the same offender. This narrative information from the offense reports is keyed into the data base's comments field to provide additional information to detectives doing the search, so that the are not just relying on the responding patrol

---

[4] When the CPD's new computer-aided dispatch (CAD) system comes on-line in a few years, all patrol officers will have computers for immediate entry of case reports.

officers' categorization of incidents.[5] This use of the narrative information is one of the most important distinctions between MAPADS and RAMIS. In fact, detectives who initially were skeptical about MAPADS because they felt it was primarily a mapping system became enthusiastic when they learned about MAPADS's capabilities.

One additional benefit of the crime mapping project has been increased cooperation between detectives in Area 5 and patrol officers in District 25. Skolnick (1967) and Sanders (1977) have noted that competition between detectives and patrol officers is the norm, and we also noted this. However, in this project patrol officers and detectives cooperated in teaching each other how to use the equipment, in sharing the results of their analyses, and in sharing information about crime patterns.

The benefits of such cooperation go beyond interoffice activities. After noticing a number of incidents of older women being robbed by youths around the intersection of Belmont and Central Avenues, the District 25 crime analysis officer contacted officers in District 16, whose southern border abuts the northern border of District 25 on Belmont Avenue. The combined data from the two districts suggested a pattern; on July 8, 1988, the CAU was requested to perform a pattern analysis, which confirmed the existence of a pattern in that neighborhood. On July 11, detectives were brought into the picture, and on July 21, the offender was apprehended, clearing a number of robberies. The entire process took about 2 weeks and pointed out how a capability for analysis in districts can be of benefit to detective operations.

[5]The detective working on the taxicab robbery case also learned something about categorizing incidents himself. He was the only one doing data entry and still found that in the comments field he described one of the robberies as a taxicab robbery and another as a cab robbery, which initially prevented him from tying them together using a text search. He subsequently standardized his terminology.

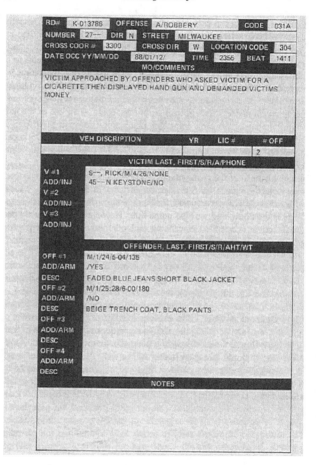

RD#	K-013786	OFFENSE	A/ROBBERY		CODE	031A

RD# K-013786 OFFENSE A/ROBBERY CODE 031A
NUMBER 27-- DIR N STREET MILWAUKEE
CROSS COOR # 3300 CROSS DIR W LOCATION CODE 304
DATE OCC YY/MM/DD 88/01/12/ TIME 2356 BEAT 1411
MO/COMMENTS

VICTIM APPROACHED BY OFFENDERS WHO ASKED VICTIM FOR A
CIGARETTE THEN DISPLAYED HAND GUN AND DEMANDED VICTIMS
MONEY.

VEH DISCRIPTION YR LIC # # OFF
2

VICTIM LAST, FIRST/S/R/A/PHONE
V #1   S--, RICK/M/4/26/NONE
ADD/INJ   45-- N KEYSTONE/NO
V #2
ADD/INJ
V #3
ADD/INJ

OFFENDER, LAST, FIRST/S/R/AHT/WT
OFF #1   M/1/24/5-04/135
ADD/ARM   /YES
DESC   FADED BLUE JEANS SHORT BLACK JACKET
OFF #2   M/1/25:28/6-00/180
ADD/ARM   /NO
DESC   BEIGE TRENCH COAT, BLACK PANTS
OFF #3
ADD/ARM
DESC
OFF #4
ADD/ARM
DESC

NOTES

Figure 7.1. Example of a free-form text field for
and abstract of narrative information on the computer

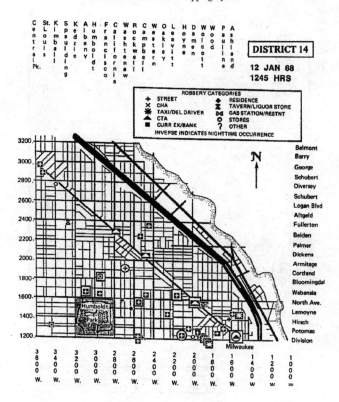

Figure 7.2. Map that indicates pattern
of armed robberies of cab drivers.

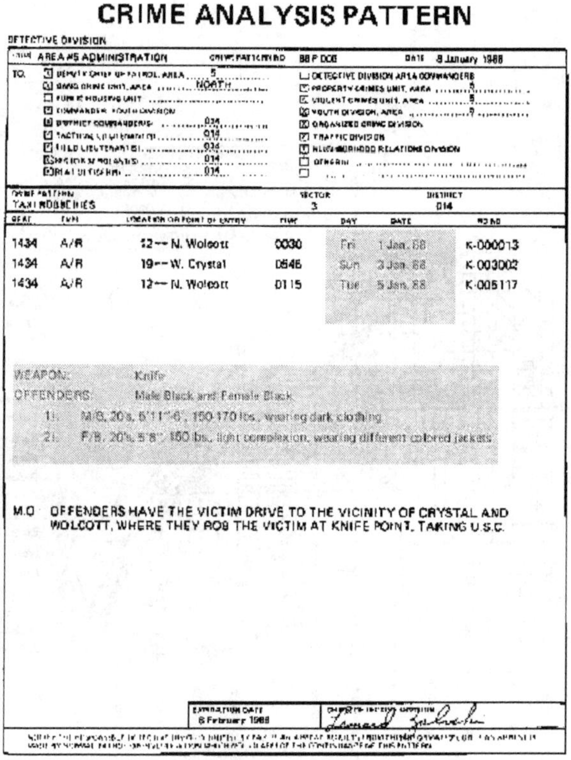

CRIME ANALYSIS PATTERN

DETECTIVE DIVISION

AREA #5 ADMINISTRATION — CRIME PATTERN NO. 88 P 006 — DATE 8 January 1988

TO:

- DEPUTY CHIEF OF PATROL, AREA 5
- GANG CRIME UNIT, AREA NORTH
- PUBLIC HOUSING UNIT
- COMMANDER, YOUTH DIVISION
- DISTRICT COMMANDER(S) 014
- TACTICAL LIEUTENANT(S) 014
- FIELD LIEUTENANT(S) 014
- 014
- 014
- DETECTIVE DIVISION AREA COMMANDERS
- PROPERTY CRIMES UNIT, AREA 5
- VIOLENT CRIMES UNIT, AREA 5
- YOUTH DIVISION, AREA 5
- ORGANIZED CRIME DIVISION
- TRAFFIC DIVISION
- NEIGHBORHOOD RELATIONS DIVISION
- OTHER(S)

CRIME PATTERN: TAXI ROBBERIES — SECTOR: 3 — DISTRICT: 014

BEAT	TYPE	LOCATION OR POINT OF ENTRY	TIME	DAY	DATE	RD NO
1434	A/R	12-- N. Wolcott	0030	Fri	1 Jan. 88	K-000013
1434	A/R	19-- W. Crystal	0545	Sun	3 Jan. 88	K-003002
1434	A/R	12-- N. Wolcott	0115	Tue	5 Jan. 88	K-005117

WEAPON: Knife

OFFENDERS: Male Black and Female Black

1. M/B, 20's, 5'11"-6', 150-170 lbs., wearing dark clothing
2. F/B, 20's, 5'8", 150 lbs., light complexion, wearing different colored jackets

M.O. OFFENDERS HAVE THE VICTIM DRIVE TO THE VICINITY OF CRYSTAL AND WOLCOTT, WHERE THEY ROB THE VICTIM AT KNIFE POINT, TAKING U.S.C.

EXPIRATION DATE: 8 February 1988

Figure 7.3. Crime analysis pattern used in the case of taxicab robberies.

CHAPTER 8

Using the Mapping System for Proactive Management

One major but unanticipated result of the crime mapping project is what we have termed *proactive management*, defined by one official as an administrator having access to data so he can make decisions immediately. Rather than having to rely on central headquarters capabilities and wait for a cumbersome mainframe computer operation to eventually provide the requisite analysis, the district commander can now delegate the crime analysis officer to do the work, receive the results that day, and make management decisions as indicated. In current management science terminology, this is called a decision support system.

In most major police departments, report preparation is reactive. That is, the types of reports that are requested from district commanders are specified by central office personnel. Because these departments are generally computerized, the computer systems personnel are charged with providing the districts (and the central office) with the reports. Thus, use of the data is overseen for the most part by data systems professionals. This situation inhibits innovative data analysis for management purposes for the following reasons:

- Not every district needs to develop the same reports–a district with a burgeoning auto theft problem would want different analyses of data than would one where the primary problem is burglary–so district-specific management requires reports to be tailor-made for each District.
- To develop new reports based on computer-collected data, a special program must be written for the mainframe computer.
- The mainframe is programmed by personnel with formal training in computer programming; such personnel are in short supply in most police departments.
- Programming and debugging for special reports often have low priority, so these reports can take weeks to reach the programmer let alone provide a manager with analyses.
- It often takes more paperwork to request a special report than the report justifies--especially when the district commander is not sure, before seeing the report, that any good would come of it.

The availability of a microcomputer in District 25 changed this picture. The district commander took a proactive approach to managing his resources, providing his superior officers and subordinates with information they would not have been able to consider had only the mainframe computer been available, for the following three reasons:

- The analyst was a tactical officer who is computer literate (for example, he has a personal computer at home), but who had only a few hours of training on the machine and software and whose other "formal" training consisted of reading the software manual-thus, no specialized manpower was needed.
- The computer was dedicated to the district's business by virtue of its location and the requirements of the grant, so reports for the district commander had high priority.
- Most important, when the district commander had an idea of the type of analysis or report he wanted to see, all he needed to do was to go next door and request it from the analyst.

The following views of the district commander about MAPADS and its implementation in his district are instructive:

The first community meeting I attended after I became district commander was held at Steinmetz High School. Although I was new to the job, I knew enough to know that I needed to find out what the crime picture was in the community. So I spoke to the detectives working upstairs [in Area 5], because I knew that they could get what I needed. The meeting was 10 days away, but they said, "You're not giving us enough time, it takes about 2 weeks." But I was in a bind, and they got it for me. I later found out that it was on the computer and that it shouldn't take that long.

I looked at the list of crimes and it shocked me at the amount of crime these people had to put up with. So I was on the defensive, especially after the meeting started and six or seven people stood up and told horror stories. I was in an indefensible position. Later, though, when I looked at the printout again, I saw that it wasn't as bad as all that. It's just that the amount of time and the size of the area were so large that it showed the area to be much worse than it really was.

When [the computer] came I didn't know what it could do but Marc [Officer Buslik] was so effective at using the system that he taught me what I could get out of it. It was really great at the very next meeting with a community group. It was at a church in Kelvyn Park. I asked Marc for a printout of the crime. I had no idea I would get a map; I thought I would just get a list like the last time but in less time. But I got both the list and the map. So I went to the church armed with it and it showed them that they really didn't have a crime problem, and so let's talk about what their problem really was.

Well, it turned out that what they were really upset about was people having sex in cars, parking in the alleys, dope selling in a house (and those cases are hard to make), and cock fighting in the park on Sundays. It took us some time, but we were able to take care of these things for the most part.

The crime mapping project produced a potential new role, that of crime analysis officer. Crime analysis officer is not a formal position in the CPD but rather the title given to the officer in the district who was assigned to work on the MAPADS project.

Appendix D describes the duties of such a position for departments that wish to institute such a system as a regular part of their organization. The role of the crime analysis officer is an expansion of the review officer role. In the CPD, the review officer, under the direct supervision of the district commander, is responsible for assembling, evaluating, and retrieving case reports and other official incident documents regarding reported crimes and calls for service.

There are two review officers in District 25. The crime analysis officer was detailed from his assignment as a tactical officer to the new role. Creation of the crime analysis officer role reflected a broader shift. The mapping capability allowed the district commander to do analyses not previously possible at the district level. Subsequently, he was able to use such analyses to make manpower allocation decisions and to provide intelligence and feedback to his officers. This district commander was thus the only one of the 25 in the CPD who had such resources.

Although the role of crime analysis officer was created in response to the crime mapping project, its responsibilities extended beyond that. Thus, the district commander frequently gave the crime analysis officer numerical reports produced downtown to study for possible implications for District 25 operations. For example, the crime analysis officer may try to determine if there is any pattern to the relationship of district of residence to district of arrest or examine district-by-district differentials in the distribution of Part I arrests by patrol officers and by detectives.

This analytic capability permitted the district commander to be highly innovative in using the data-data that have heretofore been largely inaccessible to district commanders. When the commander of District 25 wanted a special report, or map, or analysis done, he requested it directly from his crime analysis officer. This resulted in a whole range of data-driven activity; which included the following:

1. generating beat-by-beat productivity measures;
2. developing and mapping crime awareness bulletins for patrol officers:
3. providing beat officers with crime maps of their beats, which depicted and listed the crimes occurring over the past week:
4. developing directed patrol missions that used data, reports, and maps for concentrated patrol efforts;
5. providing narcotics activity bulletins periodically to patrol officers. with narcotics activity hot spots (identified either by police or community organizations) mapped;
6. providing gang activity bulletins periodically to patrol officers, with gang turf and major gang-related incidents (identified either by police or community organizations) mapped; and
7. providing maps and offense printouts of specific areas to the district commander, to assist him in providing information to community groups.

None of these analyses had been possible before the mapping system was provided to District 25. We consider this to be a major step forward in both police administration and crime analysis, an advance that was not foreseen when the crime mapping project was started, exemplifying the power steering concept described earlier.

Before the advent of MAPADS, directed patrol missions were planned by the tactical lieutenant. He or she might look at the statistics for the last period and see which beats were high in robbery, burglary, or auto theft and plan assignments based on that information. Then he or she might read through the case reports to get a feel for the types of cases. With MAPADS this was no longer the case, as the following quote indicates:

> Crime analysis officer: What we found was that we could spot patterns before the [downtown] crime analysis unit could. Not just geography, but type of crime pattern, too. We feel we're planning directed patrol missions in a more rational way. It's very hard to quantify, because in many instances we did not apprehend anyone but the crime did stop. They [the tac officers] learned more how to be in the right place at the right time.

An additional aspect of proactive management was the involvement of patrol officers in patrol planning. One of the difficulties we had was our naive assumption that simply providing good intelligence to beat officers would result in their using it effectively. Our interviews with and observations of patrol officers indicated a lack of understanding of what to do with the maps. Many patrol officers were as likely to use the maps as scrap paper as to keep them in their beat books for later referral. The assumption of these beat officers appeared to be that any paperwork that came down from the commander was just additional busywork.

In an attempt to rectify this situation, we identified those officers who were in fact using the maps, and we convened a series of meetings. In one of these, six patrol officers, the District Commander, the Crime Analysis Officer, and representatives of CANS, NU, and UIC had a frank discussion of the use of the maps, why they were not being used by many officers, and what steps might be taken to encourage their use. As a direct result of these efforts, the following steps were taken:

- Watch commanders began to discuss the material on the maps at roll calls.
- Patrol officers were encouraged to keep all maps so that they could refer to them.
- Maps showing the location of recovered stolen autos were produced.
- The 24-hour activity report was modified in accordance with the officers' suggestions.

There were two significant aspects to this process. First, the meetings provided a rare opportunity for command personnel and street officers to discuss problems and solutions. Second, the agreed-upon changes were implemented within 3 days, showing the officers that they were in fact part of the decision-making process. By building such flexibility into a large bureaucracy such as the CPD, the organization becomes more responsive to changing local circumstances. In fact, this type of input by patrol officers is a key component of problem-oriented policing.

Proactive management faces outward as well as inward. The District 25 commander found that one of the major benefits of the mapping technology concerned community relations. In particular, from an administrator's vantage point, decentralized computer mapping of crime gave him much greater capabilities and credibility in rumor control. In the past, administrators were sometimes caught flatfooted at community meetings when residents complained about certain incidents. With MAPADS, a police manager can have more timely, focused information and can correct inaccurate accounts; defuse potential conflicts between community and police; and even take the initiative in providing block-level, offense-specific, current information to residents. This community relations capability impressed some police managers as perhaps the most significant achievement of the crime mapping project thus far.

CHAPTER 9

Police-Community Cooperative Use of MAPADS

The technological advance represented by computerized mapping constitutes only part of the potential benefit of MAPADS. To be truly effective, MAPADS needs to work in an organizational and social context that permits the police and the community to interact while analyzing the data. This interaction requires trust and practice as well as an organizational and social infrastructure. We expected this infrastructure to be developed as the police and the community used MAPADS jointly in working on problems of crime and safety in the community. This did occur: the project made an important contribution to the development of this infrastructure. Cooperative working relations were established and information was exchanged regularly between the community and the police. This was an important achievement of this project.

When we initially contemplated the joint use of the system by police and community, we had a specific product in mind. The icons on the map that represent crimes were to be surrounded by icons that represent incivilities. The incivilities were to be contributed by the community, the crime data by the police. The information was to be shared in working sessions, which were to be held on a regular basis and during which the police and community crime analysts would search for patterns in the data, with the police contributing their general knowledge about offender behavior and the community contributing their specific knowledge about community conditions. This joint effort would create a context of community-police dialogue in which crime and crime-related community concerns would be better understood and handled.

Although this was (and remains) our goal, it did not occur on a routine basis during the course of the project. However, other instances of cooperation between the police and the community with respect to crime mapping did occur. One major area in which cooperation was generated, and which set the stage for continued cooperation, was in the production of crime maps. Other instances of cooperation were closer to the joint analysis effort we had originally envisioned; two examples, related to hot spots, are detailed in this chapter. However, they were not part of a regular sharing of information; they were responses to specific problems brought by community residents to community meetings attended by police administrators.

This chapter describes the benefits that are produced by the cooperative efforts of the police and the community. We wish to emphasize that in the crime mapping project communication, cooperation, and data provision flowed in two directions. That is, not only did community organizations and residents provide the CPD with data and perceptions regarding crime and other hazards but in addition, the following occurred:

- Community organizations shared with the CPD their expertise in computer mapping, which they had started some 2 years earlier.
- The CPD provided crime data to community organizations in a form that enabled them to reanalyze the data on the organizations' personal computers.
- In his meetings with community organizations, the district commander provided them with maps showing the recent crime experience of the community.
- Directed patrol missions were based in part on the perceptions and analysis of community organizations.

Although the maps were to be a vehicle for joint activity as an end product, it turned out that the process of producing the maps was also instrumental in bridging the gap between the different perspectives on crime and disorder held by the police and the community. In the next section we describe how producing the maps served as a common ground for the police and the community to work together. Following that, the manner in which the police and community cooperated in their efforts to reduce crime and incivilities is described (particularly with respect to two hot spots), as is the use of maps by other community organizations.

Producing the Maps

The maps were more than just a graphic tool for analysis of crime patterns. They were tools coproduced by CANS and the CPD, which helped to build an atmosphere of trust. Because of this, the maps were also catalysts to action even where information could have been presented in another fashion.

The first step in the process was drawing the base maps. The maps were manually entered into the computer by CANS because its staff had a great deal of experience in this activity.[1] CANS based the computer maps on the paper maps obtained from the City of Chicago Planning Department. After CANS completed them, the maps were revised by the District 25 crime analysis officer.

[1]The map production effort was facilitated by the fact that the streets in Chicago are laid out on a rectangular grid along the points of the compass. Manual entry of maps will not be necessary for other departments, because computerized street layouts for most large cities are now available from a variety of sources.

The second (and ongoing) step was producing the maps containing the crime data. We had originally expected to produce them in the same manner in which CANS had produced maps for its other projects: CANS was to receive the monthly crime data tape provided by the CPD and take it to Northwestern University for mounting on its mainframe, where its format would be converted and the data downloaded to diskettes for use on the Macintosh computers at the CANS office.

It quickly became apparent that monthly maps, which were for the most part adequate for community organization concerns about hot spots and persistent patterns, would be totally inadequate for the police. A new production system was designed, based on the 24-hour activity reports. As described in Chapter 5, 24-hour activity reports were converted from paper reports to computer- produced reports generated by the same data. The District 25 review officers entered the crime data daily into the microcomputer.

However, after the crime data were stored in the data base, they had to be manually linked to a map. This step, which is tedious and time-consuming (and will be unnecessary in the future because new software can perform it automatically), was also performed by CANS staff on a weekly, then biweekly, basis. At first the disk was transferred to CANS via interoffice mail from the district to the downtown headquarters, where a CANS staff member picked it up (see again Fig. 6.1). At the CANS office, the symbols representing the crime were placed on a map manually and linked to the crime incident information. When finished, the printed maps, the crime incident reports, and the disk with the maps and data were sent back to District 25. Eventually, modems were installed at the district and at CANS, and maps and information were sent back and forth electronically. Production of the maps using these procedures became a reliable routine.

The process was not always smooth. Neither party built the production process into its routine immediately, and a break with routine at one end made planning at the other end difficult. Initially this problematic production process was also complicated by flaws in the interoffice mail distribution in both directions. Despite the problems of start-up, CANS and the district jointly produced maps for 12 beats containing a monthly average of 263 incidents. In addition to sending the maps to the district, CANS sent relevant biweekly beat maps to six community-based organizations. One of these organizations, in addition to receiving the beat maps .based on the daily activity output from District 25, received crime maps based on the department's computer tape with its more comprehensive record of reported crimes, which included drug arrests.

The process designed to produce maps required compromise on the part of both parties. District personnel had to give time to the production in order to get maps in a more timely fashion. CANS had to forgo receiving the broader range of crime information of interest to the community organizations, including information about narcotics arrests and arrests for prostitution contained on the computer tapes it had been using in its mapping.

Using the Maps

The maps were extremely useful as a method of transmitting complicated information to community organizations. They were used by the district commander in presentations to community meetings and by the community in presentations to the police. For the commander they were a good briefing tool, and the graphic presentation helped him make his points. For the community groups, they were not only a graphic way of communicating, but they were also a more powerful tool because the maps made community residents' concerns tangible and concrete to the police and were a professional and polished means of transmitting their concerns.

To provide an understanding of the way the maps were used jointly by the police and community organizations, we will describe two specific instances of their use, both relating to what the community saw as hot spots. The first hot spot was a retail commercial corner at the intersection of North and Central Avenues. The second was a suspected drug house on Lotus Street. Both are in the area served by the Northeast Austin Organization (NAO), the most active community organization involved in the crime mapping project and a member of CANS since its early days. NAO serves the residents of 90 blocks in the southeast corner of District 25. This area is highly organized, with approximately 30 block clubs.

NAO uses the maps in a variety of ways. NAO staff members often bring the crime maps to block watch meetings; in addition, the maps are used in recruiting on an ad hoc basis. The major routine use of the maps is for rumor control; it is the experience of some NAO staff members that people tend to think the worst, and the maps are a useful tool for reassuring residents.

Other community organizations received and used the maps as well. Their use of the maps is described below.

The North and Central Hot Spot

Austin, one of Chicago's 77 community areas, is a community in racial transition. Between 1966 and 1973, blocks changed from white to black at a rate of 37.5 per year (Taub, Taylor, & Dunham, 1984). This transition has slowed, but it can be postulated that many of the whites who remain are too poor to leave and many of the blacks moving into Austin also do not have the resources necessary to move out of the community. The residents want to make it safe to walk the streets and come and go from their homes without worrying about muggers, rapists, or even panhandlers. At one block club meeting a resident said, "Let's face it, this is the last of the last. Unless you win the lottery this is where we are going to be. We have to make it work here. There is nowhere else to go."

The businesspeople in the Austin community share the residents' aspiration for a safer community. They want to be able to operate a business without worrying about being held up, victimized by shoplifters, or assaulted. They feel that patrons should not be afraid to approach their businesses because it appears dangerous to do so. However, the business conditions in Austin often do not represent the ideal.

One of the hot spots identified by NAO is at the corner of North and Central Avenues, a busy intersection of two major arteries. It is the site of two all-night stores (a fast food store and a convenience store), a currency exchange, and a liquor

store. It was nominated as a hot spot at several community meetings, where fears
about this corner were volunteered by residents, as in the following examples:

> Jim: When I was in there [a local convenience store] there was a guy wrestlin' with one of the
> employees and another guy swinging around a broken bottle. Finally, one of the other workers
> went and got a baseball bat and had to hit the guy.

> Sue: It's really hard to run a business when that kind of thing is going on. We are trying to cut
> down on the shopliftin'. . . We make people leave their shopping bags at the door... We only
> let 5 [people] in at a time at night. It used to be that winos would come in and drink our beer
> in the store.

People expressed concern with drug dealing ("I've been watching the parking lot
of the [fast food store] at night and I've seen them passing dope for money from one
car to another") and robberies; they felt unsafe going there ("They let them sit out in
the parking lot and party all night ... all sitting on the hoods of their cars and eatin'
and drinkin' and smokin'; they got their little, no, those big radios playin' and just sit
out and party all night"); and said repeatedly that the fast food store was being used
as a hangout for robbery crews that look for likely victims getting off the bus or
shopping at other stores in the area.

It is a physically attractive business intersection but has a higher than normal crime
rate and-as we later discovered--a much higher rate of calls for (disturbance) service.
It is feared by residents at certain hours, by merchants at other hours. Because the
area is developing a bad reputation, it is vulnerable to competition, and the fragile
health of the business strip and the neighborhood may be injured if progress is not
made on the hot spot. Without a solution, the area could become a victim of
disinvestment, become run-down, and produce more disorder and crime.

This assessment of the intersection was not initially shared by the police. It was
their contention that crime at the North and Central intersection was not any different
from that at the corner of North Avenue and Pulaski Road, 2 miles to the east. The
initial mapping of the situation tended to ear this out. Thus, the police did not see the
intersection as a major police problem, but were willing to respond to the
community's concerns, as the following comments indicate:

> Officer 1: What it appears we have here is a fear of crime which the people hanging out at these
> places inspires.

> Officer 2: It's a perceived thing. If I walk into a [convenience store] and there are six guys
> standing there playing video games it makes me nervous.

> Officer 3: The people here are looking to the police to solve a social problem. I'm not sure it
> is ours to solve. All we can do is listen to their requests. If it's reasonable we can allocate
> resources; if not, we will have to say it does not represent that great a police problem. This is
> certainly not a gross problem. Maybe they need to get in touch with other city agencies. It's a
> social problem which maybe the police can help with.

In spite of the initial response by the police representatives-that they did not see a police problem at North and Central based on an analysis of the data they had–the district commander acknowledged the community perceptions of a crime problem. Although this problem was outside the police definition of crime, the district commander noted that some sort of police response was possible, as the following comments indicate:

Crime Analysis Officer: Then they [the community] need to recognize that this isn't necessarily a police problem. It's a social problem.

District Commander: Everything you say is true, but we still have to respond to the perceived problem.

However, CANS had 3 months of prior crime data with which to make a more long-term picture of the area. The results of this analysis (see Figs. 9.1 and 9.2; see also Table 9.1) confirmed the fact that the concentration of crimes was higher at this intersection, especially with respect to robbery, burglary, and battery. After reviewing the subsequent, more elaborate analysis, the commander agreed that there was an actual problem at the corner.[2]

Following this analysis, a meeting was scheduled with merchants in the North and Central area. Before the meeting, the crime data were analyzed to determine the distribution of crime by day of week. Two points emerged from this meeting: First, the merchants' and residents' perceptions of when the bulk of crimes occurred differed from the results of the analysis-the data showed a higher occurrence on Mondays and Tuesdays, whereas the community consensus was that the weekends had the highest frequency of occurrences; second, the merchants had a different set of concerns than did the residents--for example, the manager of the all-night convenience store was more concerned with the late night and early morning than were the residents, who were concerned about the early evening. The reason for this difference in perceptions of when the store was the most dangerous is obviously attributable to the difference concerns of the residents and store manager. Ile residents were most concerned during the hours they would frequent the store (the early evening), whereas the store manager was most concerned with the safety of her store and employees, which she felt was most problematic from 11 p.m. to 5 a.m. What concerned the store manager and several others were the young people hanging out in the fast food restaurant-many of whom were underage, "doing dope," and violating curfew. These youths would visit her store, shoplift, and disrupt and verbally (and physically) assault the store's employees.

To pursue this matter further, we examined the CFS data. We had previously obtained a tape of the 15,000 calls for service for District 25 for the month of June

---

[2]Note that the district commander did not have the same data analysis resources available to him as did CANS. The crime mapping project changed that; with MAPADS the district commander was able to proactively perform such analyses, as discussed in Chapter 8.

1987. We selected from the tape the data of greatest relevance to the issue: disturbance calls of all types, suspicious person calls, and citizens calling for help calls (see again Fig. 2.2 for the codes for these incidents). In addition, we compared this corner with that at North and Pulaski, the comparison corner mentioned previously. As can be seen in Figures 9.3 and 9.4, the number of such calls at North and Central was considerably higher than at North and Pulaski; moreover, the bulk of the disturbance calls occurred on the weekend, in consonance with the perceptions of the community, not with the crime data.

In response to the community, the district commander posted cars on the corner at the times the community had claimed the situation was the worst. There is evidence that some of the community perceived the problem solved. At a meeting of the businesspeople a month after the meeting with the police. a representative of a convenience store on the corner made the following comment:

I wanted to say about the police, whatever you folks said to the police it has really worked. The past four Sundays the police have been escorting people right down the block... They have been around all the time since that last meeting, so whatever you said to them they are doing something... They really seem to be trying.

The Lotus Avenue Hot Spot

As with the previous example, the first step in the process of promoting police-community cooperation over the Lotus Avenue hot spot involved bringing the police and the community perceptions of the problem into closer agreement.

A map of community-identified drug hot spots was assembled and shared with the district police. According to the crime analysis officer, the police were aware of about half of the hot spots. This coincidence was taken by the police as a sign of the reliability and usefulness of the map and the community-generated information. One of the targets identified was a suspected drug house on Lotus Avenue.

This two-flat house had been the focus of neighborhood attention since January 1988. Heavy traffic both on foot and by car (at all hours of the day and night) and loud weekend parties were sources of concern. Strangers were seen to knock on the front doors or on the basement windows, stay for a short time, and then leave. Several cars regularly pulled up in front of the house, and a large plastic bag was usually taken out of the trunk and carried into the house. This activity made many of the neighbors suspicious that they had a drug house on their block. They discussed the matter with a community organizer.

The community organizer attempted to enlist the residents in developing a plan of attack jointly with the district police. However, the situation was complicated. The residents' anger and disapproval were mixed with sympathy and concern for the building's owner, an elderly man who had a drinking problem and who had apparently become attached to the young women who used his house for drug sales and prostitution. The residents' anger and annoyance at the activities on their block; concern for the owner, who was himself apparently a victim; and fear of retaliation if they took action were mixed with feelings that even if they talked to the police nothing would change.

Nevertheless, along with CANS, the community organizer and 10 residents from the block met with the district commander, the neighborhood relations officer, and two beat officers. The map of drug houses compiled by the community organization was presented to the commander. The Lotus Avenue house was on the map.

At this meeting the neighbors related their concerns about the house. The police asked questions, searching for specifics, narrowing the time range of the activity, and asking for descriptions and license numbers of cars. After the meeting, the district commander commented enthusiastically on the richness of the information exchanged at the meeting and how unusual it was for the police to receive such good intelligence. The meeting adjourned with a commitment from the commander to follow through, a description of the process the police would follow, and a plea for patience.

After the meeting, the neighbors provided police with several license plate numbers, car makes, and descriptions of passengers in the cars. According to the sergeant involved in the investigation, the house has been searched 10 times, with the cooperation of the owner. The police confirmed many of the neighbors' perceptions. According to the police, the women were using drugs and evidently selling small amounts of cocaine. The police were convinced of this not because they discovered drugs but because they had seen the paraphernalia of cocaine use; however, they did not see the scales and bags associated with volume sales. "The women are turning tricks," according to the officer. "We sent two officers, but the women wouldn't do business with someone they didn't know."

The police confirmed the neighborhood residents' perception that the owner of the building was an alcoholic. When sober, lie would complain about the activities going on in his house and wanted the women and their associates out. When drunk, he didn't care. In either case, he would not sign a complaint. Part of his reluctance apparently stemmed from the fact that one of the women was his common-law wife. Another part was fear. He had been beaten up by the group that had taken over his house and they had, at least on one occasion, taken his pension check from him,

Differences in perceptions had arisen between the police and the neighbors. The police tended to view the house as disruptive to the neighborhood, but small-time and marginal as police work. As one resident commented, however, the women not only do business with men they know, but also "they're flagging cars and trucks" at a nearby intersection and "working Cicero Avenue." There has also been, for the first time, reference to a wholesaler, someone who supplies several houses in the area. One neighbor was willing to let her house be used for police surveillance. There were clearly more steps to be taken before the enforcement strategy exhausted all options.

Nevertheless, there was a feeling that the neighbors had to meet to consider other strategies, such as pressuring the owner over building code violations. At the time this volume was being written, the house's activities were continuing. The "crashpad," house of prostitution, and probably small-time drug house continues to upset neighborhood residents. The enforcement strategy has been frustrated to date.

The following is a postscript about the Lotus Avenue house from Commander Casey:

The community came in and talked to us about the Lotus Avenue problem. We got a lot of good information from them, something we hadn't gotten before; originally we had a skeptical attitude toward whether we could use their information as probable cause.

We knew that the occupants were using, but there was no indication that they were selling--no scales, no cutting material, no packaging material. So we were stuck. Then we finally made some good purchases at Lotus. sending a young female officer in and she made two hand-to-hand buys. She gained the confidence of the female who was selling to her, and found out about another drug house on Bloomingdale.

It really goes all over after that. From the Bloomingdale house we got information on a house on North Avenue. where we made a 16-gram purchase. Then to two locations on Lockwood, then to two other places on North. We ended up spending over $5000 for buys, but made a dozen arrests for dealing and four related on-view arrests.

Then to top it off came some information on guns. In fact, they gave us information about a man carrying a gun, standing on the corner of North and Long, and he was there just where they said he would be.

These two examples of the use of the mapping system point out some of its ancillary benefits. The community organization's use of a map in providing the police with information about drug houses made the provision of this information concrete; often the police are confronted with pleas for help that lack the specificity that a map provides. MAPADS was also the vehicle whereby the police and the community jointly developed strategies for dealing with a multifaceted problem. Putting drug houses on the map also permits the district crime analysis officer to determine whether or not there are any relationships between them and other crime or incivility activity in the neighborhood; as was shown in Figures 4.3 and 6.7, this is not an unwarranted assumption.

Use by Other Community Organizations

CANS distributed maps regularly to five community-based organizations and one public elementary school. Although CANS staff met with each recipient group at least three times and oriented them on the use of the maps, except for NAO the recipients were basically on their own as to how they would use the maps. Under these circumstances, the unaided users of the maps (especially those such as the Burbank-Luther Elementary School, Neighborhood Housing Services, and Northwest Austin Council, which had no previous experience with them) utilized the maps primarily for monitoring trends in the neighborhood.

At the Burbank-Luther Elementary School, for example, the crime maps were received by the principal. The principal is a beat representative, that is, a member of the community who participates in a CPD program to provide a liaison between the local police district and those who live or work in the community. He made copies of the maps for interested teachers and posted them on the bulletin board in the main office. The school is located in a low-crime area of the district, adjacent to tracks that provide a barrier from the higher crime area to the south. The maps are seen as a preventive tool, a way of monitoring events and providing an early warning mechanism. So far, they have only been used for general interest purposes.

If the amount of crime or incivilities increases, or if a pattern starts to emerge, the principal plans to follow a routine he established earlier in response to an increase in incivilities, including abandoned cars and illegal dumping. At that time a notice was sent home with each child, the school's PTA called a special community meeting, the police were notified and cooperated with the residents, and the problems were cleared up.

Another recipient of the maps was the Northwest Neighborhood Federation (NNF). NNF is made up of eight separate neighborhood areas, 720 city blocks and approximately 400 block watches.[3] Using color-coded pins and information from CANS's maps, once a month NNF staff transfer the information to their own large bulletin-board maps, one for each of their eight neighborhood areas. Then they use the bulletin-board maps at their block watch meetings. There are two reasons for the transfer. The CANS maps are divided by police beats, whereas the community group needs maps divided by the neighborhood areas. In addition, the large bulletin-board maps are more appropriate for use with groups.

The bulletin-board maps usually show only auto thefts, burglaries, and robberies because these crimes are prevalent and because they can be dealt with effectively through the block watches. NNF considers drug houses, narcotics sales, and other crimes either as too frightening for people to face (so they will not want to become involved in the block watch) or as not amenable to a quick resolution (so people's excitement and interest in the block watch will fade). In other words, block watches have to be marketed to the community, and each community has a different set of concerns.

The maps help the block watches and community organizers spot crime patterns. For instance, according to the organizers, lately there has been an increase in personal crimes-handbag snatchings and assaults. And there are always high numbers of handbag snatchings near known drug houses. The maps also help to alleviate community residents' fear of the unknown. If people have no definitive information they assume the situation is worse than it really is. The information provided on the maps gives community residents a realistic understanding of the crime problems in their neighborhoods.

Other community organizations have not had the same amount of technical assistance, nor do they have computers available (as does the NAO). Consequently, they have not been able to use the maps to the same extent as NAO. The use they do make of the maps, however, demonstrates another value the maps offer to such low-tech organizations: The members are provided not only with a list of offenses but

[3]Not all of these blocks are in District 25.

also with a map showing their locations, information that gives them an immediate
feel for the true extent of crime in their communities.

Table 9.1. Comparison of crime data at two intersections in the Austin
community

	North and Central Avenues			North avenue and Pulaski Road		
	Hotspot	Total	Percent of total	Hotspot	Total	Percent of total
Burglary	12	79	15.2%	6	82	7.3%
Robbery	15	76	19.7%	9	72	12.5%
All crime	38	264	14.4%	25	278	9.0%
Number Of blocks	8	56	14.3%	8	64	12.5%

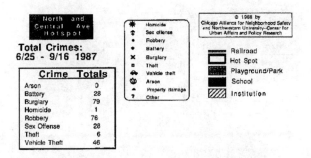

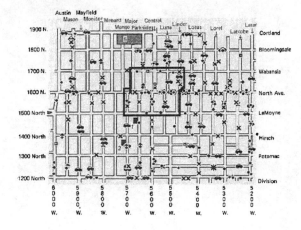

Figure 9.1. CANS analysis of crimes at the
intersection of North and Central Avenues.

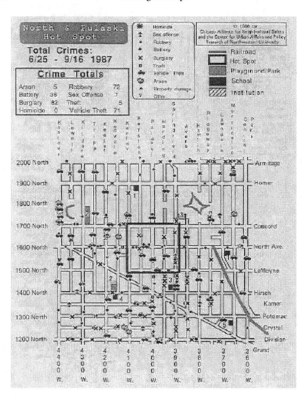

Figure 9.2. CANS analysis of crimes at the
intersection of North Avenue and Pulaski Road.

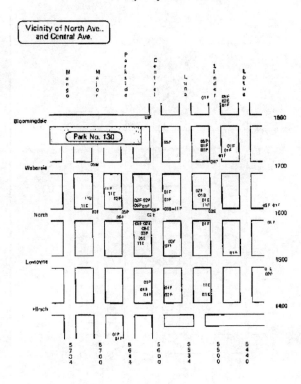

Figure 9.3. Map showing calls for service at the
intersection of North and Central Avenues.

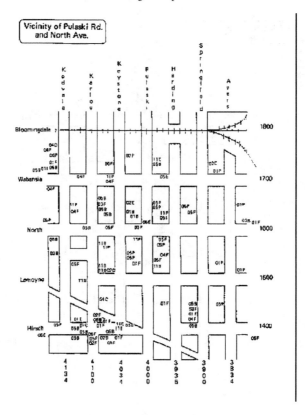

Figure 9.4. Map showing the calls for service at the
intersection of North Avenue and Pulaski Road.

Part III

Open Questions

During the course of the crime mapping project, MAPADS made its mark in District 25, in the Area 5 violent crimes unit) and in community organizations. It has been shown to be a valuable tool in the following ways:

I. For spotting crime trends;

II. For improving the chances that a patrolling officer will make an on-view arrest;

III. For reducing (or displacing) crime by permitting the district to plan more accurate and timely directed patrol missions;

IV. For permitting detectives to enter narrative information and thus augment the geographical pattern analysis with MO factors;

V. For providing community-based information to the police to assist in the more rational allocation of patrol resources; and

VI. For providing police-generated crime data back to community organizations to permit them to plan more appropriate countermeasures (e.g., block watches) and to give them a more realistic understanding of crime in their neighborhoods.

In short, we have provided evidence that MAPADS was a success in this implementation of the concept. There are, however, some important issues that this project has not addressed, issues that are crucial to extending the project beyond this pilot implementation.

One of the most important issues not addressed so far relates to the future of police-community cooperation. What we have shown in this volume is that a working collaboration between the police and community organizations can have a real impact on crime, incivilities, and neighborhood safety in a community. Those of us who were the most doubtful of the wisdom of a close collaboration are now convinced that it has been one of the most significant features of the crime mapping project. As one initially skeptical officer said, "I only wish there was some way that we could be sure of getting this type of information from the community on a regular basis." Institutionalizing this cooperation is not a trivial issue; it is discussed in Chapter 10.

A technological innovation such as MAPADS cannot be absorbed by a large organization without giving a great deal of attention to how it will affect the organization. Earlier we discussed the way in which the reward structure of a police department needs to recognize the value for patrol officers of solving a problem by means other than arrest and, for detectives, of sharing credit when one detective's information helps another to clear a crime; this is another aspect of problem-oriented policing. There are broader implications for the organization, too; they are discussed in Chapter 11.

The focus of most police work on Part I crimes to the exclusion of subcriminal antisocial behavior is imbedded in the issue of community-police cooperation. One of the ways in which police attention to these subcriminal incidents can be improved is to move the beat officer away from this single focus and to use incivility data to help direct his or her patrol strategy. Although some of this information can only be obtained through contact with community organizations, a great deal of information is already collected by police departments but is currently unused by them for the most part: CFS data. A difficulty in including calls for service on a map is the volume of incidents that would then clutter it up. One means of getting around this information overload is to portray the incidents dynamically, that is, to show the incidents as they occur in their time sequence. In that way one could show 24 hours of activity by displaying 24 frames in sequence, each showing the activity occurring in an hour; it would also be possible to display 96 frames of 15-minute segments. Furthermore, additional contextual data could be displayed, permitting the analyst to incorporate them in a cognitive assessment of a community's safety problems. Issues concerning the implementation of this innovation are discussed in Chapter 12.

A number of additional issues arose during the course of the crime mapping project. They relate to the reasons for the improved communications that were found to exist during its implementation and the advisability of creating a new position of crime analysis officer; they are discussed in Chapter 13.

CHAPTER 10

Institutionalizing Police-Community Cooperation

Our experience with the North and Central hot spot provided us with a deeper understanding of the intricacies of the police-community-crime-incivility nexus. In an attempt to obtain a profile of this hot spot, a community organization staff member was trained to work with merchants to record events they did not report to the police. Preliminary analysis of the data made it clear that crime in the area of North and Central is a complex problem. The intersection is situated in an area where racial diversity and the close proximity of middle- and low-income people can feed fears among residents and potential investors. Finding a solution requires more than the collection, analysis, and mapping of data. Strategies based on the experience of merchants, residents, and police must be devised. These strategies can only come out of a coordinated planning process that involves all relevant parties. Gains in the area can only be maintained if the basis for action is cooperative. This need for a nontraditional problem-solving approach suggests a team response, consisting of police officers and community representatives. The task is unfamiliar for most police agencies and cannot be handled in the course of normal patrolling duties.

The question of institutionalizing police-community cooperation goes beyond the question of institutionalizing the use of the maps. It is quite possible to picture a police department using the maps without sharing them with or showing them to the community. It is also possible to picture a scale of cooperative uses ranging from showing maps to the community only at presentations to the partnership of equal sharing that has been taking place in Chicago. One-sidedness can run the other way also, as the Chicago experience makes clear. After access to police data was established, many of the groups that received maps showed them to the police only occasionally, if at all. In the context of the crime mapping project. the question of institutionalization addresses the question of the organizational and social context in which the mapping system is employed. It is a question of the community setting in which the maps are used.

As we have indicated elsewhere, the philosophy underlying the crime mapping project has focused on the importance of involving individuals significantly in decision making. This has been reflected in the development strategy for the mapping system, in the emphasis on a power steering approach over an autopilot approach, in the significant role assigned to the community as a full partner in the project, and in the maps' use as an educational tool as well as a tool for analysis. It is also reflected in the general vision we have of police-community cooperation.

For years, citizens have been told that the police cannot do their job without the cooperation of the community. In some form or another, "Be our eyes and ears" has been the slogan repeated most often. In general this appeal has not worked. Although crime regularly scores high among citizens' concerns in polls-and taxpayers continue to show their concern about crime by spending significant portions of the urban budget on policing (in Chicago, over $300 million a year)--cooperation between citizens and the police is often spotty and inadequate.

Our vision begins with a rejection of the eyes-and-ears philosophy for the same reason that the autopilot philosophy was rejected: the need for full involvement of the community. If residents are perceived and treated as tools, as the mere scanning and listening devices that this image implies, fuller cooperation will never be achieved. Residents should watch and report, but this is not an adequate definition of their role. Police should recognize that community residents see things from a different contextual standpoint than do the police. Just as effective crime analysis requires the intelligence, feelings, knowledge, and intuition of the analyst, effective cooperation requires the *full* participation of citizens as equal partners. By *equality* we mean equality of status, not of role and function. But most police interaction is with individuals, often victims who put in calls for service, and there is no possibility of even a roughly equal partnership between individuals in crisis and a large public agency. There is not only an inherent inequality of power but also little if any mutual accountability and only a fleeting match of interests.

Partnership can only exist in a situation in which parties with a sustained mutual interest can hold each other accountable for delivery on their part of a contract. To the degree that safer neighborhoods are the goal of policing, a partnership must be developed with community organizations and institutions that share that goal and have resources to reliably commit to crime prevention and other partnership activities.

The Houston Police Department's perspective is suggestive. The department is driven by values that include the delivery of police services both in a manner that not only preserves but also advances the principles of democracy and in a manner that reinforces the concept of neighborhoods. As CANS (1988) has pointed out, "it seems clear that both the cause of democracy and the concept of neighborhoods are best carried forward in the context of a proactive, organized and purposeful community. Only in this context can the mix of services and investments needed to improve the quality of life be sustained".

The crime mapping project has shown that such a partnership can be developed and maintained between police and community organizations. But such partnerships do not spring up of their own accord. There are a host of barriers to developing the kind of mutually supportive working relations between the police and the community that must be overcome if progress is to be made toward long-term cooperation. These barriers include the following:

Incident-driven policing. Incident-driven policing creates a context that is not receptive to the development of positive, long-term partnership relations between residents and police. It suggests a highly centralized structure focused on the incident instead of on the community problem that generated it; using this strategy, making communities safer is a less important goal than is clearing individual incidents. Whatever the slogan calling for resident participation, incident-driven policing makes cooperation peripheral to police work. As has recently been pointed out by CANS (1988), Chicago not only has an incident-driven police force, but "in terms of the percentage of calls for service to which cars are dispatched, Chicago ranks highest in the nation, dispatching cars to 65-67 percent of the calls. This compares to 47 percent in New York and 26 percent in Los Angeles" (p. 25). This high rate of dispatch, often for minor or noncriminal matters, requires officers to be in their cars and out of touch with community concerns.

Distrust. The conditions created by incident-driven policing, which leave officers and residents out of touch, have sometimes allowed the distance between them to fill with distrust. Distrust must be overcome before real cooperation is possible. In our experience, this is a slow process that depends on sustained personal contact and the mediation of those who have gained the trust of both parties. The fact that UIC had well-established relations with the CPD, and NU had well-established relations with CANS made the project possible in the first place. Subsequently, after CANS established a strong relationship with the CPD on its own, it was able to act as a go-between for the CPD and community organizations, having gained the trust of both parties.

Organized citizens. Increasingly, policing must focus its resources on working in a problem-oriented mode with community organizations. The relationship must be sustained, it must be task- and problem-oriented, and it must have room for community participation in target selection. The relationship must include mutual responsibility for problem solving and must be designed so that the capacity of community organizations is increased to better enable them to maintain the safety of areas where the problems have been reduced. We recognize the fact that not every city has communities as well organized as the communities in Chicago. This has made the task much easier to accomplish in Chicago than would be the case in other cities. This does not mean. however, that the strategies outlined here will not work in other cities. In fact, the police are instrumental in developing community organizations in other cities, and these organizations would doubtless not start off with the legacy of confrontational politics that had been the case in Chicago between the CPD and some community organizations. Thus, mutual trust may be easier to achieve elsewhere.

Coordination of agencies. As the examples of North and Central and Lotus Avenue hot spots illustrate, problem areas are complicated. Problem solving can often be facilitated by coordination with other agencies, such as the Department of Housing, the Park District, and the State's Attorney's Office. This coordination can be handled by community organizations concerned with the overall health of the community.

This would place the requests for resources in the community and avoid the jurisdictional battles that often result when one agency makes a request of another. *Funding of community efforts.* If achieving safer, less fearful neighborhoods is a socially agreed-upon goal, then crime prevention and partnership-building efforts in community organizations must be funded. There must be an investment of funds in this other half of the partnership and a commitment to building expertise among citizens for upholding their part of the contract. This funding should be used to strengthen the crime prevention activities of multi-issue organizations that are concerned with whole health of the community.

CHAPTER 11

Implications for Evaluation and Training

A technical innovation such as MAPADS fosters a great deal of change, in both the police department that implements it and the community that the department serves. The manner of implementation can change the way the police relate to the community and the way they perform their routine patrol work. These changes should affect both the way the innovation is evaluated and the way police officers are trained. This chapter discusses some of the issues raised by considering the MAPADS system as an integral component of a police department.

Implications for Evaluation

Although the MAPADS project is of great benefit for police administrators, other groups can also benefit from it. There are two elements of its philosophy that point in this direction: (a) the emphasis on links to the community and (b) the focus on making it useful for line officers, not just for administrators.

How do such benefits relate to developments in planned change in policing? What implications do they have for evaluation efforts? We can begin to address these questions in terms of Rumbaut and Bittner's (1979) observations on the directions of recent police reform efforts:

Police reform in the 1970s has become an established enterprise, increasingly under the technical and administrative control of a class of professional change-makers. The present direction of technologically and legalistically determined reforms reflects an accelerated movement away from concerns of "substantive rationality" to those of "formal rationality" so that the reform process has become depoliticized and lacks policy direction. While helping to insulate the police from arbitrary political manipulation, this movement also attenuates the aims of substantive political justice, including those of police accountability, local community review, and control of police discretionary policymaking powers. Moreover, the prevailing forms of change-making in police organizations have not been substantively aimed toward creating the informed, skilled and judicious police officer. (p. 239)

Where does the crime mapping project fit among such characterizations? It does appear rather apolitical, but it also creates opportunities for substantive community review. It does suggest increased rationalization of policing, but its implementation also appears to be consistent with the development of more judicious police officers. Furthermore, some evidence from the experience of detectives in this project indicates that it is an energizing force. much as intensive probation supervision initiatives are for probation officers (Thomson, 1987).

However, the extent to which MAPADS will actually energize and promote police professionalization will likely depend on the environment into which it is introduced. If that environment is characterized by engaged leadership, interlevel communication within the department, interactive evaluations of officers, high morale, tight police-community relations, and inclusive community organizations, this innovation should succeed in desirable ways. However, rare is the police department that can lay claim to many of these characteristics.

Furthermore, such an ideal department or district would appear to have little need for such an innovation. As in the area of court reform, we may have the paradox that reform will be carefully and successfully implemented only where it is least needed and most undermined where it is most needed (Feeley, 1983). Given the resilience of local cultures (whether community- or organization-based) and the strength of political structures, this paradox makes sense.

In the current case, it may be helpful then to ask about the prospects of the initiative in less than ideal settings. in those we might characterize as middle-of-the-road, neither automatic or tautological successes (because of its enthusiastic and innovative acceptance) nor automatic or tautological failures (because of its rejection as a waste of time). To do so requires that evaluators address some broader issues. These might include questions such as the following: To what extent do community organizations' interests in greater cooperation with the police by use of the maps represent exclusionary interests (e.g., maintaining racial or ethnic segregation)? To what extent do these interests represent a desire for tranquil communities within the context of an inclusive society? To what extent do they represent a desire for local community autonomy and citizens' control of their lives? The active partnership of the CANS umbrella in the crime mapping project promises that the cooperative efforts of the project will be guided toward intergroup respect, but what might happen elsewhere should be a matter of concern.

There is another set of questions evaluators might address to respond to the concern raised by Rumbaut and Bittner about contributions of current police reform efforts to substantive rationality. One subset might focus on the extent to which this innovation empowers individual officers in their work, reducing the us-versus-them feeling between the patrol officers and the command staff. The following subset would assess how the initiative guides policing: Is the result a crackdown on juvenile garage burglars or on rapists? Do police officers increase enforcement, order maintenance, or service activities (Wilson, 1968)? For what types of offenses do clearances increase? Is there a displacement effect, with other clearances decreasing? Any such differences might be explained situationally, organizationally, or environmentally. But for an evaluation of this technological innovation to be more than merely technical and if it is to consider the political and ethical implications, such questions must be addressed. Then the description and explanation of differential policing consequences will be material for community involvement in the sense of debating what the community wants police to do.

Implications for Training

There is a need to differentiate training according to type of unit. Although this will vary according to the dynamics and needs of individual departments, there seem to be enough commonalities in policing, especially in larger departments, so that differentiating training by functional divisions (i.e., uniformed patrol officers, tactical officers, detectives, and administrators) can be considered a general principle.

Patrol Officers

Management and field detectives enthusiastically, and fairly extensively, received and used the mapping technology. For the management, it provided community relations, patrol allocation, and morale-boosting capabilities. For the field detectives, it bolstered crime-patterning capabilities and, through the inclusion of computer-accessible case narratives, augmented individual and organizational memory and facilitated cooperation among investigators. It also fit in well with the ethos of the detective division, with its public role as the creative and innovative investigator making optimal use of all resources.

The public role of the patrol officer is strikingly different from that of detectives or administrators; consistent with this, patrol reception and use of mapping was also strikingly different. Most uniformed patrol officers seemed to make little use of mapping (or of other investigative capabilities of the organization for that matter) and tended to be quite derisive of it. The most vocally expressed attitude was "A good cop knows his beat."

Such behavior and attitudes reflect the different roles of patrol officers and detectives. The former patrol assigned areas, respond to radio calls, and serve an order maintenance function, whereas the latter conduct crime investigations, in which they enjoy a fair amount of autonomy. Those members of the patrol division with responsibilities most like those of the detectives–that is, the tactical officers–made much more use of the crime mapping system and were very positive about it. Their mission areas were based on map analyses, and they were in and out of the review office (where the computer was located) all the time, whereas no more than a handful of the district's 250 uniformed patrol officers were ever in there. Although maps and the various alert bulletins were distributed at roll calls, generally little if anything was said about them; they rarely made it into the beat book; and, as one committed official wryly suggested, they may have been used mostly as scratch paper by patrol officers. However, as a result of these observations, based on interviews early in the crime mapping project's life, the maps have been emphasized more at roll calls and officers now keep them in their beat books.

Is it even worthwhile to invest in mapping training for patrol officers given the above characterizations? Even if mapping is inappropriate for patrol officers (which we doubt), its apparent success as defined by administrative, detective, and tactical responses suggest that it is a worthwhile policing innovation anyway. So perhaps we need not be too concerned about patrol receptivity to date. Before leaving the matter, however, we will take a closer look at the dynamics of patrol officers' receptivity--or lack thereof-and how we might interpret it.

Officers themselves accounted for their lack of use of the maps by noting such factors as the radio-responsive nature of their work, the geographic size of the district, the department's manpower shortage, dispatch practices that result in often being called out of their beat assignments, and some lack of constancy in beat assignments. Note that many of these factors are district- or department-specific.

It is unclear how the issue of beat assignment relates to MAPADS. On the one hand, in departments with personnel, dispatch, and allocation policies and practices that put the same officer in the same beat every day and throughout his or her watch, mapping might be perceived as considerably more useful and hence received more favorably. To the extent that such a department emphasizes community or problem-oriented policing over radio dependency, the attractiveness of mapping will be enhanced still further. On the other hand, it may be that the maps are even more useful in departments in which beat assignments are *not* permanent; as previously discussed, the maps can serve as the institutional memory when an individual officer's memory is incomplete.

There is also a project-specific explanation for the problem of patrol hostility. We did not provide sufficient training, and adequate software was lacking. In particular, the computer program that we used did not allow the analyst to show the patrol officer more than one beat on a map. With improved software, this problem will be eliminated.

A broader explanation for patrol response to mapping relates more directly to police culture, in terms of cynicism and xenophobia, and to work-group dynamics in general. It is common for members of the same organization to talk disparagingly about superiors, subordinates, or other outsiders. It happens with students and faculty, junior faculty and senior faculty, and faculty and administration. Certainly, it happens with patrol officers and detectives, officers and brass, and administrators and community groups. Some of the patrol officers' reactions to mapping might thus be discounted as so much routine complaining or ritual grumbling, exacerbated in the patrol setting by the very real potential for danger, coupled with the perceived lack of public appreciation and a natural disdain of outsiders. This may be especially true when the designated academic researcher attends roll call and asks officers for their opinions of the maps. If only a handful of officers use and appreciate the technology, they are not going to speak up when other officers are knocking the maps to the researcher.

This analysis and other information garnered during our research suggest four implications. First, focus on the small number of advocates. Identify them and nurture their interest. The meeting of the district commander with half a dozen interested and involved patrol officers was a promising beginning along these lines in District 25.

Second, be patient. The supporters may be found primarily among the younger and newer officers (as are some of the most vocal of the detractors) and the "good cops." The others are likely to be impervious to most sales efforts. Instead, one must depend on a long-term socialization, aging-out, and recruitment process. The District 25 commander, for example, expects that it will take 5 years before mapping will be adequately used by his patrol officers.

Third, be circumspect. Taking a cue from Niederhoffer (1967) and years of police culture research, one should ensure that the realities of patrol partner assignments do not sabotage incipient interests in mapping and other innovations. Pairing a mapping enthusiast with a cynic may convert the cynic, but the odds may be against this outcome.

Fourth, emphasize the experiential. One veteran officer reported that when he was on the street lie saw little value to mapping but that after being given an opportunity to see it in operation he recognized its value. There might be some value then to providing such firsthand experience to more officers. Perhaps this even implies some broader management innovations, such as some job rotation.

All of this suggests that it may be necessary to look harder and be more modest in expectations with regard to mapping utility for patrol officers. For example, despite the expected routine grumbling about (and rejection of) an imposed innovation, even negative officers interviewed in the crime mapping project conceded a place for mapping for geographically patterned crimes such as auto theft and burglary rather than crimes of opportunity such as purse snatches. Engaging even recalcitrant officers in discussions of the system elicited suggestions for improvements ranging from ordering the 24-hour activity reports in some useful way for information retrieval (e.g., alphabetically) to distributing maps showing place of recovery of stolen autos or showing both place of theft and place of recovery to help specify directionality.

Administrative Training

Even among responsible administrators in this project, there was a perception at an early point that maps were being distributed at only some of the roll calls. Not only does such distribution require timeliness, but it also requires consistent and committed follow-through. And the follow-through must be unwavering. It is not enough for the district commander and the crime analysis officer to be committed to the innovation. Their commitment and vision must percolate through the chain of command so that patrol officers are not receiving the message that this initiative is fair game. Consequently, watch commanders and supervising sergeants must take it seriously and be perceived as taking it seriously.

This means, in part, that mere distribution of the materials is not enough. Administrators need to explain the maps and bulletins and their potential usefulness. As some officers suggested, these officials should take 10 to 15 minutes at roll calls to walk through the mapping materials with their officers. But for this to be effective, the managers have to be sold on the innovation and be conversant with its capabilities.

To make sure managers know the system's capabilities will require taking some time with the managers to show them what the system has done and can do. Such administrative training must pave the way for experiential training for patrol officers, for downward percolation is not enough. Bringing potentially interested officers in, by ones and twos, to the crime analysis office for a 20-minute hands-on demonstration of what the system can do, especially what it can do for them, is one means of moving in this direction. Paying more attention to disseminating successful uses of the systems is another way. In a large decentralized organization, with major structural and cultural sources of resistance to top-down and external innovations, eternal vigilance is the price of effective communication. A high degree of redundancy in communicating mapping results may be necessary for there to be much hope of denting the consciousness of officers absorbed in other demands and routines.

There does then seem to be some promise for greater receptivity, although it may take considerable time and persistence before the requisite training, socialization, and administrative commitment pay off. Whether such a level of commitment is desirable is a major policy question for each department considering such a mapping system. For some, the less costly benefits available in the administrative, detective, and tactical areas and the less obvious benefits to be realized in the patrol area may be arguments for leaving the latter alone, at least for the time being.

Tactical Unit Training

During the crime mapping project, the one operational segment of the patrol division demonstrated noticeable enthusiasm for mapping was the tactical unit. Tactical officers may be thought of as patrol officers in plainclothes, but they are also something of a hybrid between patrol officers (although that is their classification) and detectives. Tactical officers enjoy more autonomy than uniformed patrol officers, focusing on vice and narcotics problems in the district, and they perform preliminary investigations before detectives get involved. More often, though, their missions involve patrolling designated areas, known as directed patrol missions, and sometimes staking out suspected drug houses or other suspect scenes. They are not radio-responsive as uniformed patrol officers are; they have a work situation more conducive to the use of the mapping project products.

They use the maps. During the project individual tactical officers stopped in regularly to the crime analysis office to request further information relative to a lead or a pattern. Large maps denoting the directed patrol areas for the period are posted on the walls of the tactical unit office where the tactical officers regularly gather for roll calls and paperwork. The assignments were determined by the district commander and crime analysis officer based on their assessment of the maps. The beat with the highest number of burglaries during the preceding period was thus specified as the burglary directed patrol mission for the current period. The same practice was followed with regard to robberies and car thefts. Tactical officers concentrate their uncommitted time to patrolling these areas.

Thus, we do not anticipate that tactical officers will require much in the way of convincing that MAPADS is of benefit to them or training them in their use. Since their "beat" is district-wide, the maps help to orient them quickly to their latest target area.

One overriding suggestion seems clear from the conduct of this project and others in the burgeoning area of policing research: If the innovation is to be used by a specific group-patrol officers, tactical officers, detectives-bring that group in on the project from the beginning. Don't let this become an us-versus-them situation. If they participate in the implementation of the system, they will be more inclined to make sure that it flies. Although not all of the users are going to be interested in making it work, a top-down implementation will be resisted all the more.

CHAPTER 12

Incorporation of Additional Data

At the moment, there are two primary types of data collected and displayed by MAPADS. The first type is the geographical data: the streets, blocks, railroad tracks, and so on that make up the portion of the city being displayed. The second type is crime data: type of crime, location of the crime, and time of occurrence. In addition, when information about hot spots or other safety problems are provided to the police, these are also mapped.

There is a great deal of additional information, however, that can be displayed on a map that would be of benefit for crime analysis purposes. Data on incivilities, for example, can be extracted from CFS data. The computer can be programmed to display crimes dynamically, in chronological sequence of their occurrence, so that patterns in time can be displayed by MAPADS. Similarly, land use, weather, traffic, and transit schedule data can be superimposed on the map to permit the analyst to determine how these variables might affect crime. Even more to the point of police-community concerns, a community calendar of events can be integrated into MAPADS to permit the analyst to determine how they affect safety.

Calls for Service Data

We made preliminary analyses of CFS data to determine the extent to which patterns of interest to police and community organizations can be inferred from them. Our initial exploration of these data led us to recognize their value for mapping purposes; aside from having such uses as finding repeat complaint addresses (as has been done in Minneapolis. Newport News, and Boston), these data have intrinsic value in helping to describe community concerns that may not achieve the threshold of criminal activity. Although there currently is a delay of approximately 2 to 3 days before the dispatch cards are entered into the mainframe computer, this does not appear to be a major stumbling block to operational use of the data in the CPD for the following two reasons:

- Because one of the primary uses of these data will be to determine the existence of chronic conditions in a neighborhood, the fact that the data are a few days old should not pose a major problem.
- Because the calls for service resulting from criminal incidents are entered into the system within 1 day (via the 24-hour activity report), the remaining, less serious calls for service need not be entered immediately.

At present, CFS data are rarely used for tactical or patrol planning purposes. The addition of these data would enhance MAPADS, even if they are only available after a 3-day delay. Mapping them would allow integration of the information available from the CFS data (such as the concentration of calls of various types) with the geographically based strategies currently employed by both the district police and the community organizations. Although there is quite a high volume of CFS data, the fact that they are spread over a large geographic area keeps their mapping within the capabilities of a mapping system. By contrast, a statistical analysis would require aggregating the data to the beat or district level, and would lose the grounding in the neighborhoods that we have emphasized throughout the project.

These preliminary observations concerning the utility of the CFS data are supported by their use in the joint police-community analysis of the hot spot at North and Central Avenues, described in Chapter 9. It should also be mentioned that the CPD has begun the procurement process for a computer-aided dispatching (CAD) system, for implementation within the next few years. With CFS data captured automatically on the computer at the time of the call, the current delay will be nonexistent in the future. Incorporating CFS data into the current system, even with a delay of 2 or 3 days, will permit the CPD to be better prepared for their use of the CAD system.

Dynamic Mapping

As currently implemented. MAPADS is a static mapping system; that is, it displays whatever incidents are selected but does so in the order in which they appear in the data base. Of course, it is possible to sort the data base chronologically, so that the incidents appear sequenced in time, but even when this is done the map still fills up with all of the incidents in the data base. A *dynamic* map, as we conceive it, would show the incidents in chronological order, but the older incidents would be removed from the map, eliminating clutter and permitting the observer to get a feel for chronological-spatial incident patterns. In this way the activity in a neighborhood (or a police district) unfolds frame by frame over time. This is an innovation in crime mapping that would enhance crime analysis capabilities considerably.

For example, suppose an analyst notes that 10 minutes before a liquor store is robbed at one end of a police beat, an unfounded complaint (e.g., "man with a gun") draws the beat officer to the other end of the beat. To find out if this is a decoy operation, the analyst could search through the data base to find similar robberies, then play back the half hour prior to these robberies to see if this represents a pattern. A similar situation might exist with respect to the hypothetical high school basketball game and subsequent offenses described in Chapter 4. If a time-based dynamic map permits the area's events (end of the game, occurrence of the incidents) to unfold over time, an analyst could easily tie the incidents together.

Time-based information can be displayed on a dynamic map so that, for example, a user can watch a playback of events over a period of time in order to make inferences about relationships. The map shown in Figure 3.3 has 29 events displayed on it. Showing these events sequenced in time would contribute to finding any underlying patterns. Where a static map can only show accumulated data, animation can isolate phenomena that occur in bursts, at certain times, or only in conjunction with other events. A single address that produces many calls for service-as in the Minneapolis Repeat Complaint Address Policing (RECAP) experiment-would be shown as a throbbing sore on a dynamic display, whereas on a static display these events would be overwritten on each other. Pierce. Spaar, and Briggs (1984) analyzed patterns of repeat calls to the Boston Police Department. The Boston Police sometimes found it difficult to determine that calls emanated from the same address, because sometimes the full address was given, other times the intersection, and so on. Putting the events on a map would eliminate this problem. Although mapping itself permits the crime analyst to apply cognitive data analysis to spatial patterns, being able to watch the unfolding of activity over a period of time would extend this ability to the generation of hypotheses about space-time patterns.

Aside from this advantage, dynamic mapping also makes more manageable the potential problem of too much information. Considering that the number of calls for service in a single Chicago police district can run over 15,000 per month, portraying all of them on a map would overload an analyst's ability to comprehend any patterns. When one parses this volume of calls by hour and beat, however, the number becomes much more manageable; a district with 12 beats would average fewer than two calls per beat per hour, a number that can readily be assimilated by an analyst.

A user might display crimes that occurred during a specific time period, their locations noted by symbols (icons) of a shape or color appropriate to each crime. The analyst could choose to display the locations of vandalism, graffiti, or other incivilities and to highlight community hot spots, such as drug houses or street corners that are dangerous at certain times of day.

Mapping Other Data

Aside from mapping calls for service and other events chronologically, the MAPADS system could be enhanced as an analysis tool by including additional types of contextual data. For example, a clock on the map could show time of day and level of ambient light; an icon in the corner could display the weather at the time. Land use characteristics could be distinguished by color. Transit vehicles could be shown on their routes, especially at night (when they are most likely to be on schedule and when the perceived danger of being victimized is highest).

Displaying all of these data at once would merely clutter the screen. The user would not be able to process all of the information simultaneously but could choose which information to display and in which order, an advantage of the chronological display feature. Any subset or combination of information could be selected; for example, all rapes after dusk, all disturbances after high school basketball games, or all purse snatchings in a geographic area. Moreover, the information could be displayed showing the social context surrounding the events.

By *social context* we mean the routine activities of a community: hours that stores are open, times and locations of sporting events and meetings, times that movie theaters let out, and so on.[1] When studying crimes, police detectives gather information about the behavior and movements of offenders in an attempt to identify the offenders and solve the crime. By and large, information gathered about the behavior and movements of others (including the victims) is not used unless it will help to identify the offenders. This information, however, is of use in determining the circumstances under which the crime occurred, for crime prevention purposes. It is helpful in explaining why a particular crime took place in a particular location. Patterns of activity that may not be apparent when looking only at variables directly related to the crime may reveal themselves when the social context of the crime is known.

Although it was not possible to implement this innovation during the crime mapping project. we recommend that it be included as a major feature of the mapping software packages that are currently being used and adapted for use by police departments throughout the country. If properly implemented, it should improve a department's crime analysis capability considerably; it should also improve a community's safety.

For example, if crimes occur when community events abound, it may be that the particular types of events generate the wrong kind of traffic; too many offenders and/or too many victims may be created by the events, without the leavening effect of potential witnesses or deterrers. Conversely, if crimes occur when there are no community events, perhaps some events could be created during those periods to improve community safety.

These are but some examples of the types of data that can be integrated into a mapping system and of some of the benefits that might accrue from their integration. Note that we are not dealing with blue-sky possibilities-the innovations we suggest are well within the state of the art in both hardware and software.

[1]Our "routine activity" refers to the activity within a community, not to the routine activity of individuals within the community-for example, victims (Felson & Cohen, 1979). However, there is a strong relationship between the two, and our approach is consistent with that of Cohen and Felson.

CHAPTER 13

Thoughts on Communication in Police Departments

The discussions in earlier chapters all demonstrate the importance of the flexibility of the MAPADS system. Because such flexibility is built into MAPADS, the organization becomes more responsive to changing local circumstances. One of the important characteristics of crime analysis is that the particulars of a given case, the facts that make it solvable, do not remain the same from case to case. The similarities between cases are mostly unusable in solving cases. By developing sets of routinized procedures, an organization intended to solve crimes may inhibit its own abilities to do so. To increase effectiveness, the organization must be able to adapt to the particular circumstances involved, both on a case-by-case basis (which is the reason for street-level discretion) and on a slightly more general basis, such as concentrating on auto thefts at one time and burglaries at another (which is the reason for command-level discretion). In order to make these adaptations, field units need access to contextual data about local conditions, and they need to be able to analyze that data in a changing variety of ways. These are exactly the benefits MAPADS provided the district personnel and was beginning to provide area detectives.

Recent literature on organizations (e.g., Piore and Sabel, 1984; Sabel, 1982; Walsh, 1988; and Stinchcombe, in press) strongly suggests that decentralized decision making increases the effectiveness of an organization that faces constantly changing circumstances. A decentralized organization takes advantage of the knowledge of its workers, enabling it-to adjust quickly to local circumstances. It is most effective when circumstances vary in different areas of organizational responsibility and over time, as is the case in most urban police departments. By increasing the capability of street-level officers and detectives to respond to changing circumstances, MAPADS permits a police department to react appropriately and effectively to the wide variety of conditions encountered in urban departments.

Mapping seems to provide a benefit beyond its utility as a mechanism for depicting data in a more comprehensible manner. It also seems to have greatly facilitated communication between groups that were not especially known for communicating in the past, namely, community groups and the police, and patrol officers and detectives. There may be a number of reasons for this, such as the existence of the project, the use of maps, the sharing of information as an inherent aspect of the microcomputer implementation, and a change in police receptivity to outsiders.

The existence of the project. The improved communications experienced during the conduct of the crime mapping project may merely have been a consequence of the "Hawthorne effect," the halo effect that often accompanies a new program; that is, the fact that this was a showcase project may have meant that all of the participants wanted to put their best feet forward and behave somewhat better than they would normally.

Although this certainly had some effect on the conduct of the project, there were doubtless other reasons. The project itself served as a sort of filter: Those who were interested in it and its possibilities came into the project office, saw what was going on, and stayed to get involved; those who were not interested did not come in again. And the people who were interested were doubtless more receptive to opening up lines of communication between the different units involved.

Furthermore, although this was an experimental project, it was also integrated into the day-to-day operations of the district for more than 18 months. Thus, its experimental status was not even considered when, for example, the head of the tactical unit came in to get a quick update on the status of narcotics hot spots or on other specific problems. Although we do not totally discount the possible Hawthorne effect, we feel that it may not have been the primary reason for improved communications.

The use of the maps. The maps themselves may have been the cause of improved communications. The map is a much better communication device than is a list of offenses; for the purpose of communicating the crime characteristics of a community, the old adage, "One picture is worth a thousand words," is certainly the case. Moreover, maps facilitate the interchange of information between groups with different backgrounds because they force the parties to be specific with respect to location and type of crime. Because the dialogue about neighborhood safety is as much about the spatial distribution of crime as the frequency of crime, the use of a geographic medium for exchanging information helps both the police and community organizations pinpoint hot spots and focus their efforts on them. With regard to both of the hot spots discussed in this report (North and Central, and Lotus Avenue), the maps served to focus the discussion on specifics and were an effective means of transmitting information between the two groups.

Microcomputer implementation. The implementation of the system on a microcomputer may also provide a partial explanation for improved communications. The fact that a community organization can receive crime data from the police on a diskette makes it more likely that the community organization will use the information and feel more inclined to provide information to the CPD. Furthermore, the user-friendliness of the microcomputer makes it easier for individuals with little past experience in computers or data analysis to understand the data, to ask questions about what they see, and to share their ideas and additional information about crime and policing.

In addition, the relatively low cost of this MAPADS implementation (under $2,500 for a complete system of microcomputer, software, and printer) puts the system within reach of many community organizations. The ability of these organizations to obtain police data in a usable form and to provide data back to the police greatly facilitates communication. It also empowers the community, because the community members now have the information they need to organize and activate community responses to crime problems in their neighborhoods. Thus, a microcomputer implementation facilitates the police-community partnership vital to maintaining community safety.

Receptivity to outsiders. Over the past few years the CPD has become increasingly more receptive to developing ties with community organizations and representatives. Starting with its Beat Representative program in the 1970s, the CPD has attempted to increase the flow of information from residents and community organizations to assist in preventing crime and apprehending offenders. In addition, the CPD has also begun to experiment with new ways of policing. In this case the experimentation has included the provision of information from the CPD back to the community. As a result of this research (and other initiatives by the CPD and community organizations), receptivity to communication with community residents concerning crime has grown considerably.

Regardless of the reason(s) for it, increased communication has been a major and beneficial by-product of the crime mapping research. The fact that there is now a much greater measure of trust between former antagonists cannot be ignored. This trust has also extended beyond the period of the grant itself; although it is too soon to determine whether they will be permanent, new relationships of trust, respect, and cooperation have been forged that appear to be the harbingers of things to come. The maps may have merely been the catalyst, but they are appreciated for this result as well as for their intrinsic value.

Another result of the crime mapping project has been the recognition of the utility of the role of geographic crime analysis within a district. In conjunction with MAPADS, the crime analysis officer augmented the functions of review officers. The primary duty of the crime analysis officer was to provide analyses for the commander, which included maps for special patrols, for tactical officers, and for gang and narcotics enforcement. The crime analysis officer is akin to a research analyst in the branch office of a corporation who does not have the capabilities of the headquarters research department but is able to service the needs of the branch office that may be peculiar to that branch.[1] Such a role should be considered, either as a separate position or as part of the review officer function.

The primary skill required of the crime analysis officer is a familiarity with MAPADS and ancillary software, including data base management systems and some statistical

[1] One of the first projects of the Law Enforcement Assistance Administration in the 1960s was to experiment with civilian operations analysts in the CPD. The current project has some of the earmarks of that early attempt to provide police with an analysis capability.

procedures. This will enable the officer to know what questions the system can answer and how to get that information out of the system in a form suitable for its intended use (e.g., maps, bar charts, lists of offenses, etc.). The officer would also have the duty of producing maps for patrol officers on a regular basis and of developing new reports as needed, such as gang awareness bulletins, narcotics awareness bulletins, and special advisory bulletins. He or she would also perform analyses for beat and tactical officers on an as-needed basis.

The position of crime analysis officer may be a mixed blessing. It is certainly more efficient, in terms of training, to have only one person responsible for the above tasks; furthermore, it is also better for only one person to filter all of the reports and therefore have an overview that, if shared by more people, would be more restricted in scope.

Such a concentration of knowledge in one position, however, may bring about a return to the computer expert problem discussed in Chapter 8, wherein only certain individuals are knowledgeable about the computer's capabilities and are effectively the system's gatekeepers (see French & Raven, 1968). This was one of the problems that the implementation of MAPADS addressed. If general access to the system is not permitted, the system doesn't benefit from the input of various users, who may have different views on what data should be collected and which reports generated, as well as on how to design the interface between the computer and potential users. If the crime analysis officer leaves or is transferred, a great deal of specialized information is lost, and it may take a long time to train a replacement. Furthermore, access is limited to the times when the officer is on duty, which would tend to limit the system's effectiveness, especially with regard to the availability of MAPADS to assist officers on the midnight shift.

However, if access is unrestricted for anyone with a minimum of computer expertise who wants to play with the data, there is then a strong possibility that the integrity of either the data or the system might be endangered. A balance needs to be struck between the need to ensure system integrity by limiting access and the need to promote widespread use of the system by facilitating access. It may be worth it to consider having a number of crime analysis officers in each district, perhaps up to three to permit coverage through vacations, or to combine the job with that of the review officer. It may also be worth it to consider an additional role for the crime analysis officer: providing MAPADS information directly to patrol officers for support of their patrol activities. In this way the expertise of the crime analysis officer would be shared while providing additional information to patrol officers about conditions on their beats.

Appendices

APPENDIX A

Memorandum of Understanding

This Memorandum of Understanding is entered into between the Chicago Police Department (CPD); the Center for Research in Law and Justice, University of Illinois at Chicago (UIC); the Center for Urban Affairs and Policy Research, Northwestern University (NU); and the Chicago Alliance for Neighborhood Safety (CANS).

Whereas, the Chicago Police Department is charged with the responsibility and mandate to provide law enforcement and related services for the City of Chicago, Illinois; and

Whereas, the Center for Research in Law and Justice, University of Illinois at Chicago, is an institution with technical expertise in law enforcement and computer-related research; and

Whereas, the Center for Urban Affairs and Policy Research, Northwestern University, is an institution with expertise in research on community crime prevention strategies; and

Whereas, the Chicago Alliance for Neighborhood Safety has a history of developing and applying community crime prevention strategies, and of training in these strategies;

Be it understood that these four organizations agree to work in concert in the research and design of a computer mapping system which will improve the means of analyzing crime and incivility data by police and community organizations.

The terms of this Memorandum of Understanding are subject to approval and allocation of funding for the proposal entitled "Mapping Crime in Its Community Setting." This proposal has been submitted for funding consideration to the National Institute of Justice. Should the proposal be rejected, it is the intent of the parties that they not be bound by the terms of this Memorandum.

The terms of this Memorandum of Understanding are subject to, but not limited by, the following terms and conditions:

- The research, as proposed, represents a multi-year effort for all parties.
- End products of this research will include crime mapping systems usable by the CPD and other police agencies, and by CANS and other community organizations.
- The CPD retains the right to control utilization and deployment of police resources.
- The CPD will have responsibility for and control over all data entry on CPD premises.

151

- All parties recognize the CPD as being the repository of official crime statistics for crime reporting and crime statistics purposes.
- Development of the definition of "incivility" data will be a cooperative effort of all parties.
- CANS will gather and enter the incivility data on computers, will be responsible for its quality control, and will be the repository of such data during the life of the project and after its termination.
- Grant reporting will be centralized in the CPD, which will retain overall budgetary oversight, in keeping with NIJ guidelines.
- Selection of the pilot police district(s) will be a cooperative effort of all parties. All parties agree to develop and coordinate reliable and timely methods of data transfer.
- All parties will review all publications associated with this research prior to submission for publication. All publications will acknowledge it as a joint project of the parties to this Memorandum. Parties to this memorandum who disagree with the content of proposed publications will have the right to have a disclaimer incorporated in the proposed publication.
- Press releases will be considered publications for the duration of this research project.
- All resources received by the parties to this Memorandum in connection with this project, including hardware, will be dedicated entirely (100%) to this project.
- All parties will participate equally in program development for this project.
- All parties agree that the proposed studies which emanate from this project are potentially beneficial and will support such studies as part of this project.
- This Memorandum is not intended as a substitute for ongoing cooperation.
- The terms of this Memorandum are not intended to represent a comprehensive listing of the duties and responsibilities of the parties. The parties recognize that the nature of this undertaking dictates a flexible approach to interorganizational cooperation.

APPENDIX B

Hardware and Software Considerations

When the crime mapping project began there were few alternative computer systems to choose from among for implementing a crime mapping system. Our intention was to place mapping and analysis tools in the hands of experienced police officers, crime analysts, and community residents who were knowledgeable about crime prevention and well acquainted with their neighborhoods. We did not want computer expertise to be required for effective system use.

Mainframe mapping systems have been available for more than a decade, but they were so expensive and required such arcane knowledge that they met almost none of our criteria. The centralized mapping systems already in use in the city of Chicago, although of great value to computer experts, were so unwieldy that only a handful of technical people in the entire city government could use them. Moreover, because the existing mapping system was centrally held and managed, the city was unable to provide timely services even to the existing user pool. It was highly unlikely that the additional demands we would be making could be responded to with existing mainframe resources. Similar difficulties plagued the crime data base management system that the police department used; a small number of experts could use it proficiently, but even in offices dedicated to such analyses (e.g., the crime analysis unit) only a minority of the users understood the computerized system. When the experts were unavailable, the system sat idle.

Thus, the existing mainframe-based mapping and data base tools were wholly insufficient for our purposes. At the same time, the value of mapping crimes is apparent enough so that both police officials and community organizations had utilized pin maps from time to time. Although these decentralized pushpin maps were accessible and easily understood, they had other important drawbacks, which repeatedly led to their being abandoned. Without a link to a data base management system they were very difficult to update and to interpret. Very few crimes and very little data about crimes could be displayed at once without overwhelming the user. And it was impossible to query the maps in any detail-for example, to follow up on an apparent pattern among the pins or to look only at the crimes which occurred after midnight, and so on.

153

We hoped in this project to utilize a system that provided the best features of all these systems--a system that was inexpensive and readily available, easy to use and to understand, readily updated, and one that allowed nonexpert users to focus on and to analyze events that met whatever criteria concerned them. At its best, the system would take advantage of whatever expertise the user already possessed.

Based on our consideration of these criteria and on our previous experience with mapping systems, we chose to implement MAPADS using Business Filevision on an Apple Macintosh. Since we began the project, several hardware and software options have become available. This appendix describes the best features and most significant weaknesses of the system we implemented, and our reassessment of characteristics of an ideal mapping system for crime analysis.

Hardware

We felt that implementing a mapping system on an Apple Macintosh met many of our criteria. One of the most important features of the Macintosh is its consistent user interface. After a novice learns the details of how to run any program, from the crime mapping system to a word processor, nearly all of the skills can be transferred to any other program. In all environment where there are few computer experts but many substantive experts (e.g., crime analysts); where there is a substantial turnover or rotation of personnel; and where the software is being continually modified, it is hard to overestimate the importance of both ease of use and transferability of skills. The Macintosh pull-down menus and desktop metaphor proved to be easy for police and community personnel to learn and to use. The pull-down menus and mouse-driven report production allowed users readily to navigate their way through even the most complex commands. As we have indicated elsewhere in this volume, the transferability of skills to other applications meant that the computer was used for a variety of functions that we could not have anticipated. The ways in which computer use became embedded in the day-to-day operations of the district had a synergistic effect on various crime-related and administrative functions, including but not limited to mapping.

The Macintosh display is better suited for graphics applications than those of most other personal computers. There is a single standard for graphics (QuickDraw), which works with all Macintosh applications, monitors, and printers. There is no need to concern oneself with whether a given program requires a VGA, EGA, CGA, or monochrome display adapter and monitor, for example. The major drawback to the Macintosh was that MS-DOS running on IBM systems or IBM clones is a much more widely accepted standard in many settings, including police departments. After considering the advantages and disadvantages of these competing environments, particularly given the fact that our pilot district had no microcomputers when we began, the Macintosh remained our hardware of choice. The donation of equipment by Apple was helpful but not decisive; the visibility of the project was sufficient enough for us to have received competing donations had we sought them.

Software

It was far more difficult to select an acceptable software strategy for the mapping component of our project. Ideally, we were seeking a powerful yet flexible and easily used data base for storing crime information. We wanted the data base design to be relational so that information entered once at any level (e.g., street level) would be available for use at any other level (e.g., citywide) The system should accept data manually entered from the keyboard or electronically transferred from outside sources, such as the CPD's mainframe computer. When the address of an event (a crime incident, for example) is entered into the data base, the system should be able to check automatically to verify that the address does exist. That location should also be automatically "geocoded," or converted from the street identifier (5555 W. Grand Avenue) into an x-y coordinate on a detailed Cartesian grid (3475689, 5337645). It should also provide other geographic identifiers, including the appropriate police district and beat, community area, and so on.

The mapping component should allow maps to be created using a digitizing tablet or a mouse but should also take advantage of the wealth of existing electronic mapping data (such as the U.S. Census Bureau's TIGER files). The system must allow the storage and retrieval of a sufficiently large map. For our purposes a Chicago police district (equivalent to a medium-sized city) was sufficient, but ideally one should be able easily to manage a detailed street map of the entire Chicago metropolitan area. At best, this crime mapping system might be a full-fledged geographic information system (GIS) that would serve the needs of not only the public safety community but also all those who could benefit from geographically sensitive data. To satisfy the interactive uses that we were promoting, one must be able to display and redraw maps quickly enough so that users feel encouraged to play with the system and to explore their hunches. The system should also enable the user to zoom in to show great detail in a small area, or zoom out to show a larger area with less detail. One should be able to display an area of any shape or size. The particular information to be displayed and the amount of detail to be seen at any time should be specifiable by the user.

We sought a tightly integrated and easily understood and maintained link between the data component (e.g., crime details) and the mapping component (e.g., crime location) which would allow for the display of point-oriented crime data. The user should be able to select a subset of crime incidents for display and analysis (e.g., show only assaults from last week that occurred in the evening), and it should be easy to specify and then to respecify this list. In addition, the user should also be able to mark specific crimes on the map and read through the details of those crimes.

Crime events frequently pile up in particular locations, and the program should provide a strategy for handling multiple incidents at the same spot or, ideally, at locations within a user-specifiable geographic range of a chosen location. It should be possible to preserve the confidentiality of data as necessary (e.g., by providing approximate addresses).

Business Filevision

No available software met all of the criteria we set forth for the crime mapping project. We settled on Business Filevision (originally marketed by Telos, Inc., currently by Marvelin) as the software that came closest to meeting our needs. The data base was simple to use and provided a close link both practically and conceptually between the mapping system and the underlying event data. It also provided for easy event entry from the keyboard and could automatically read electronic data transferred from the police department's mainframe. The data base assigned to any incident was readily specified and reorganized when necessary. Icons that represented particular kinds of events (e.g., a picture of a car for auto thefts and of a syringe for drug offenses) were easily drawn and used, and readily interpreted by all users. Maps from selected data could be printed out in a format that users found useful and easy to understand. Report generation was straightforward and flexible.

However, the software had important drawbacks as well. The map area was limited to 8.5 by 11 inches (although a series of small maps could be linked to form larger maps). The database was a flat file; it lacked relational capabilities, which prevented us from geocoding addresses and automatically locating an icon on the screen. This meant that each crime incident had to be placed manually on the map, which required data entry personnel to be completely familiar with beat geography and substantially slowed data entry operations.[2] Business Filevision could not read geographic data from other systems (e.g., coordinate data from a dedicated Intergraph system), and all our maps had to be drawn by hand. Moreover, each map was in a separate file and it was clumsy to compare information across mapped areas.

Despite these disadvantages, Business Filevision proved to be an excellent vehicle for exploring the potential and the problems associated with crime mapping in our pilot project. Even given the acknowledged limitations of the software and the emergence of competitive systems over the last 3 years, Business Filevision remains a good choice for small- and medium-sized cities that want to limit their use to crime mapping. But we have decided that our single district approached the outer limit of the geographic area for which Business Filevision was sufficient and that it would be preposterous to adopt this system for a city as large as Chicago.

Business Filevision has been succeeded by Filevision IV. Although the new product solves some of the existing problems (e.g., map size), important limitations remain, including the lack of a relational data base or the ability to read geocoordinates from other systems, and so our concerns about this strategy persist.

Although this problem facilitated the cooperation between the police and community groups in our project (see Chapter 9), manual placement could hardly be described as a feature to aspire to in the long run.

---

[2]Although this problem facilitated the cooperation between the police and the community groups in our project (see Chapter 9), manual placement could hardly be described as a feature to aspire to in the long run.

MapGrafix

During the course of the crime mapping project we kept in touch with ComGrafix of Clearwater, Florida. This company had been working on a more advanced mapping system, named MapGrafix, which overcame many of the limitations of Business Filevision. ComGrafix's intention has been to build a true geographic information system (GIS) that could outperform mainframe GIS packages. We tested prerelease versions of this software and made suggestions as to how it might be made more useful for our type of project. The result of this cooperation is a system that meets most of our requirements.

A major strength of MapGrafix is that the data base is independent of the mapping system. Any data base management system that can produce a standard text file can be used, including competing relational data base management systems, flat file systems, and even spreadsheets such as Lotus 1-2-3 or Microsoft Excel. In our case, this enables us to use a more sophisticated, relational data base which would allow us to verify the addresses as the data are entered and to geocode the addresses. This ultimately allows for the automated placement of crime incidents on the map.

Second, MapGrafix allows the user to create maps that are much larger than those limited to 8.5 by 11 inches by Business Filevision and to zoom in on small areas as well as zoom out to view larger areas-all the while rigorously maintaining the location and relative scale of each object, be it a street, a building, a neighborhood, or a crime event.

The speed at which maps are drawn is still a concern with MapGrafix if one is using a standard 68000-based Mac Plus or Mac SE. Although the system is still usable, it will probably discourage the casual searches that often reveal new information. On a 68020 system (the Mac II) or on a 68030 system (the Mac IIx or IIcx), the speed increases dramatically.

Subsequent versions of MapGrafix have added additional features that add to the utility of the system, including an increasing number of input and output devices and the ability to read wide varieties of external digital maps (such as the U.S. Census Bureau's DIME or TIGER files).

The current price of the MapGrafix system is a $8,500 for the first copy; (additional copies are less expensive). Compared to Business Filevision's suggested retail price of $495, this makes MapGrafix less suitable for smaller police departments.

In fact, all of the systems we are discussing here fall in what is referred to as the low end of GIS systems-under $10,000--whereas many systems at the high end cost substantially more than $250,000.[3] The most important added benefit from the far larger systems is the ability to specify more precisely vast quantities of information (e.g., the exact location of sewer pipes and electrical lines). Our impression is that full-blown GIS systems are potentially far more powerful but require considerable coordination across jurisdictions in order for their advantages to be realized. Their

---

[3]For a recent detailed discussion of GIS, see Burroughs (1989).

complexity also requires maintaining a large staff of computer professionals and leads, ironically, to their being less available to the substantive professionals with whom we are concerned.

The price of the data base is also not included in MapGrafix's price. A typical data base will run an additional $200 to $500. We initially used the Omnis 3 Plus data base (by Blythe Software) with MapGrafix. We were able to implement the address checking and geocoding features, which allowed for the automatic placement of symbols on the maps. We are currently exploring FoxBase+ as an alternative data base. The present generation of FoxBase+ runs substantially faster than Omnis and gives us greater control over the geocoding process. FoxBase+ has the additional benefit of being portable to MS-DOS-based systems.

In summary. we believe that high end microcomputer packages such as MapGrafix offer, say. 85% of the features of full GIS systems in a far more user-friendly and affordable package.

Alternatives

Although we believe that using a the Mac 11 and MapGrafix FoxBase+ is the best hardware-software combination, there are other alternatives.

MS-DOS-Midas

The recently available Midas system seems to offer many of the same features as MapGrafix at a substantially lower cost. The graphics quality oil the MS-DOS side, however, are still inferior to those on the Macintosh.

MapInfo

The MapInfo mapping system, marketed by MapInfo Corporation, combines some mapping and data base features available in Business Revision with some GIS features available in MapGrafix in an affordable package for MS-DOS machines. Thematic maps are readily produced in MapInfo, but the link between the maps and the underlying data is less smooth than in Business Filevision, and icons cannot be as fully exploited. Although it does not offer the range of GIS features available in MapGrafix, MapInfo can import some forms of mapping coordinates and maintain consistency across geographic files. Its built-in data base component is compatible with standard dBase files. The graphics quality is inferior to that achievable on a Macintosh system, but may be sufficient for most police purposes.

Criterion

Criterion offers a package that also matches many of the features of MapGrafix. Its system is sold with a great deal of customization, which increases its cost even higher than that of MapGrafix and makes it only practical for departments with large budgets.

Macintosh-HyperCard

Apple's recently released HyperCard program can be made to function very similarly to Business Revision. HyperCard is included with the system software in every Macintosh at no additional cost. The largest single map that ran be created in HyperCard is about 4 by 6 inches. but multiple maps can be linked just as with Business Revision. Given the low cost of HyperCard and its flexibility, it is a good jumping-off place for people beginning to examine the possibilities of mapping crime data.

Caveat

While this volume was being prepared, major improvements in computer hardware and software were announced. Newer, more powerful Macintosh and MS-DOS machines and graphics-oriented software are now readily available. In addition. GIS hardware-software combinations using more powerful work stations are being used in some police departments. Although our description of available hardware and software is accurate for the moment, it is only a snapshot in a dynamic area in which new developments continue to occur.

APPENDIX C

CPD Detective Procedures Manual
(Crime Analysis Patterns)

14.12   CRIME PATTERNS AND INFORMATION BULLETINS

A. A comprehensive crime analysis system can be an invaluable aid in the
   identification of existing and emerging crime conditions which are occurring
   both within a specified area or on a city-wide basis. The publication of patterns
   of crime discovered through crime analysis can aid in both identifying offenders
   and the subsequent clearing of reported crime.
B. Definitions
   1. A crime pattern is the association of two or more particular criminal
      activities with an individual or group of individuals believed
      responsible for the crimes. This association can be made because of
      the type of crime, the method of operation, and/or the description of
      the offender(s).
   2. An information bulletin identifies a grouping of criminal incidents of
      a similar nature wherein insufficient information is available to
      determine if the same offender or group of offenders is responsible for
      the commission of the crimes.
C. The crime analysis unit (CAU) of the detective division headquarters
   administrative section will engage in systematic analysis of reported crime to
   identify crime patterns. Additionally, the CAU is responsible for:
   1. Issuing crime analysis pattern and general information bulletin control
      numbers. The control number will follow the following format:

      88-P-123 or 88-13-123

The first two digits indicate the year of issue, the third character indicates the type of document-pattern (P) or bulletin (B), and the last three digits are sequential numbers within each type of document, i.e., pattern or bulletin, starting with the number 001 for the first issuance of the year. Updated or revised patterns and bulletins will use the alpha character added to the control number, e.g., 88-P-123A.

2. Publishing and distributing crime analysis patterns and general information bulletins.

3. Maintaining a master file of all crime analysis patterns and general information bulletins.

4. Training area/section personnel in crime analysis techniques.

5. Amending crime patterns and information bulletins as new information is learned.

6. Informing department units when a previously issued crime analysis pattern or general information bulletin has been cleared by arrest.

D. Each area/section unit will engage in a systematic analysis of reported crime to identify crime patterns. Additionally, the area/section commander will ensure that:

1. One copy of each original case report received by his command is forwarded to CAU.

2. Members of his command follow approved crime analysis procedures.

3. Selected members of his command are trained in the procedures of crime analysis.

4. Copies of all related case and supplementary reports and the crime analysis cover sheet are forwarded to the CAU for review and publication when a pattern is discerned by unit personnel. The cover sheet will consist of a completed crime analysis report form containing all pertinent information on the pattern and signed by the unit commanding officer.

5. The CAU is notified when a previously identified crime pattern is cleared by arrest. This notification should take place on the day the pattern is cleared and will be accomplished by calling the CAU at PAX 0-395.

6. Copies of all supplementary reports prepared in conjunction with the clearance of a crime pattern are forwarded to the CAU within 24 hours of the clearing arrest.

APPENDIX D

MAPADS: A User's Guide

What is MAPADS ?

MAPADS (Micro-computer Assisted Police Analysis and Deployment System) is an economical, easy-to-use, computerized tool used for crime analysis. It is not a specific brand of software or hardware but consists of several generic types of programs that can reside on one of a variety of computers. The four components of MAPADS are: mapping, data base management, spreadsheet preparation, and presentation graphics.

Mapping software permits the display of symbols, or "icons," representing a particular type of incident to be placed on a map of a town, police district, or patrol beat. These symbols can be different shapes, different colors, or of varying sizes, visually indicating further details about an event. The map can be zoomed in on to great detail or exploded to show a large geographic area.

Combined with a data base management system, the mapping software can be used to display selected incidents or summaries of incidents. Sophisticated sorting of the collection of incident records can reveal patterns. Detailed reports can be prepared that provide insight into any particular trends.

A spreadsheet is used to accumulate raw statistics about incidents. By tracking the incidence of crime by predefined geographic or time variables, formulas can be used to determine where to deploy resources.

Using presentation or "business" graphics, data from the mapping/data base and spreadsheet components is used to create various types of charts. These present the information in a more readily interpretable fashion.

MAPADS is based on the concept of proactive, or predictive, analysis of crime and related trends. When analysts actively look for relationships among incidents, resource deployment decisions can be made in a rational method. This is proactive police management. No longer does a police chief or commander need to wait for a community to demand action based on their perceptions, but rather he or she can make timely deployment decisions based on observable trends and developments.

In addition, MAPADS provides field patrol officers with palatable intelligence about the community that they serve. Preventive patrol tactics can be based on actual

162

incidents, not just hunches or inaccurate suppositions. Follow-up investigators and detectives can use MAPADS to develop leads tying offenders with specific offenses fitting similar characteristics.

The community can use MAPADS as a planning tool for its own crime prevention techniques, such as Neighborhood Watch.

Who Should Use This Guide

This guide should be read by those in one of four user categories. First is the *Police Manager*. This person is responsible for setting both policy and operational requirements for resource allocation. In a small department, this will usually be the chief of police. In a larger agency, the district commander or watch supervisor serves in this capacity.

The *Crime Analysis Officer (CAO)* or crime analyst should be familiar with this guide and with what MAPADS is and can do. The CAO will usually be doing the data entry, data manipulation and report generation. Although in some systems, the original incident abstracts may be entered by someone or something else (a civilian data entry clerk, or downloaded from a larger computer to the microcomputer), the CAO will be spending considerable time working with the system.

Field Patrol Officers will want to review this guide to see how MAPADS can make their job more productive and efficient.

Follow-up Investigators or Detectives should become familiar with this guide and the functions of MAPADS that can assist them in their work.

A final note is necessary about whom this guide is not directed to. Although a basic tenet of MAPADS is to use community-based information as a component of the police decision-making process, this manual is directed only at the police user. Community use of MAPADS is not covered here.

The Police Manager

The Police Manager is able to use MAPADS in four major areas. The first is as a community relations tool. As a communicator, MAPADS fits the saying that one picture is worth a thousand words. A map makes it is easy to get across to citizens ideas about their community. This allows increased interaction and permits more intense probing into the concerns of the community when their fears do not coincide with actualities. Mapping then becomes an ideal tool for problem-oriented policing, because it assists in the identification of locations of police and community interest.

As a function of administrative review, MAPADS allows for supervisors to be made aware of problem areas within their jurisdiction, as well as effective policing techniques by examining areas that reveal little problem.

As an analysis tool, MAPADS can allow the Police Manager to work with the CAO to determine those areas that reveal trends that need to be addressed. In this way, the Police Manager can keep a finger on the pulse of the community.

Finally, as an operations aid, MAPADS allows the Police Manager to make rational decisions as to resource allocation-where to put his or her people. Response to a changing environment can be done knowledgeably and effectively.

The Crime Analysis Officer

The CAO should be a member of the Police Manager's support staff. The CAO provides analysis of trends regarding crime, calls for service, and other activities related to providing police services. Under most circumstances this unfortunately takes on a limited scope because of a lack of good information going into the analysis system-garbage in, garbage out. With good data, however, especially when data entry is automated, the CAO can begin to take on tasks that are of major importance in supporting the Police Manager.

The CAO needs to be fluent in the capabilities of all software, so that both standard and custom analyses/reports can be easily obtained. The Attachment lists the various reports to be generated by the CAO, along with the guidelines for their preparation.

The Field Patrol Officer

A basic concept of a patrol officer's duties is that he or she is to spend free time (while not on a previous specific assignment) on something called *aggressive preventive patrol*. This keeps the officer visible to the community and looking for possible criminal activity. Frequently, this patrol is random throughout the officer's beat, with enforcement efforts usually by chance.

MAPADS provides the patrol officer with good intelligence as to where this free time should be spent. Although this does not imply that certain areas are to be neglected by officers, those locales needing the high visibility patrol will get it.

The maps should become a guide to the streets, alleys, school yards, and so on. where the officer needs to see and be seen. Indicating where crimes have occurred, the maps show the general areas where new offenses are likely to take place. By being in the right place at the right time, the patrol officer will either prevent an offense or interrupt one taking place.

Charts give a pictorial representation of incident trends as they relate to geographic and/or historic reference points. Patrol officers can use these pieces of information in developing overall strategies for patrol techniques.

Reports detailing the various offenses provide key information about victims, offenders, and property. These all indicate who and what an officer should be paying attention to while on patrol.

The Follow-Up Investigator

Crime patterns that link an individual offender to a series of offenses are not easily prepared. Because of the variable nature of criminals, these patterns may not be all too plain. MAPADS provides a means of readily determining patterns based on geography. The ability to map an offense and link details about it is a great advantage in the preparation of patterns.

The ability to use different symbols representing different incidents and details about the incidents (time, etc.) permit the creation of selected crime missions for detective follow-up.

In addition to mapping, the record attached to the symbol provides for the development of a modus operandi file. These MO's can be used to search, which facilitates investigations where a suspect is in custody or has been identified as an offender in other incidents.

Suggested MAPADS Standard Reports

It is recommended that the following reports be routinely prepared by the unit assigned MAPADS. As experience is gained, it is expected that additional reports will be suggested by users.

* 24-hour criminal activity report--internal:
  Summary of crimes occurring within the previous 24 hours, for distribution to police personnel.
  Prepared daily, available by 9:00 a.m.

* 24-hour criminal activity report-external:
  Summary of crimes occurring within the previous 24 hours, for distribution to the community; contains information edited to protect privacy and confidential operations.
  Prepared daily, available by 9:00 a.m.

* Weekly Beat Report:
  Summary of incidents occurring the previous week, listed by beat. Prepared weekly.

* Weekly Beat Maps:
  Maps of each beat, showing incidents on Weekly Beat Report.
  Prepared weekly with Weekly Beat Report. High Incidence Beat Map/Report: Summary and map of all offenses of a particular type on the beat with the highest activity. Prepared biweekly.

* Crime Analysis Pattern:
  Summary and map of incidents fitting a pattern or trend. Prepared as analyses indicate.

References

American Transit Association (1973). *Vandalism and Passenger Security*. Washington, DC: American Transit Association.

Becker, H. (1967). *Culture and civility in San Francisco*. Chicago: Aldine.

Biderman, A. D., Johnson, L. A., McIntyre, J., & Weir, A. W. (1967). *Report oil a pilot study in the District of Columbia oil victimization and attitudes towards law enforcement*. Washington, DC: U.S. Government Printing Office.

Brantingham, P. J., & Brantingham, P. L. (1981). *Environmental criminology*. Beverly Hills, CA: Sage Publications.

Brantingham, P. J., & Brantingham, P. L. (1984). *Patterns In Crime*. New York: Macmillan.

Burroughs, P.A. (1989). *Principles of geographical information systems for land resources assessment*. (Monograph of Soil and Resources Survey No. 12). NY: Oxford.

Bush, M., & Gordon. A. C. (1982, July). The case for involving children in child welfare decisions. *Social Work*, 309-314.

Camaghi. J., & McEwen. J. T. (1970). Automatic Pinning. In S. I. Cohn & W. E. McMahon (Eds.), *Law Enforcement Science and Technology III* Chicago: Illinois Institute of Technology Research.

Carter, J. R. (1984). *Computer mapping: Progress in the '80s*. Washington, DC: Association of American Geographers.

Chaiken, J. M., & Dormont, P. (1978a). A patrol car allocation model: Background. *Management Science*, 24, 1291-1300.

Chaiken, J. M., & Dormont, P. (1978b). A patrol car allocation model: Capabilities and algorithms. *Management Science*, 24, 1291-1300.

Chicago Alliance for Neighborhood Safety. (1988). *Police service ill Chicago: 911, dispatch-policy and neighborhood-oriented alternatives*, Chicago: Author.

Cohen, L. E., & Felson, M. (1979). Social change and crime rate trends: A routine activity approach. *American Sociological Review* 44(4), 558-608.

Dodenhoff, P. C. (1989, March 31). Interview of Thomas G. Kobus Assistant Chief of Police, Houston Police Department. *Law Enforcement News*, XV(289) 9-14.

DuBow, F., McCabe, E., & Kaplan, (1979). *Reactions to Crime: A Review of the Literature*. Washington, DC: U.S. Department of Justice.

Eck, J., & Spelman W. (1985). *Crime analysis project. Interim report*. Washington, DC: Police Executive Research Forum.

Feeley, M. (1983). *Court reform on trial: Why simple solutions fail*. New York: Basic Books.

Figlio, R. M., Hakim, S., & Rengert, G. (Eds.) (1986). *Metropolitan crime patterns*. New York: Willow Tree.

Freidson, E. (1970). *Professional dominance*. Chicago: Aldine.

French, J. R. P. Jr., & Raven, B. (1968). The bases of social power. In D. Cartwright & Zander, A. (Eds.). *Group dynamics*. New York: Harper and Row.

Garofalo, J. (1977). *Public opinion about crime The attitudes of victims and non-victims ill selected cities*. Washington, DC: U.S. Government Printing Office.

Geertz, C. (1963). *Old societies and new states: The quest for modernity in Asia and Africa*. Glencoe, IL: Free Press.

Georges-Abeyie, D. E., & Harries, K. D. (Eds.). (1980). *Crime A spatial perspective*. New York: Columbia University Press.

Goldstein, H. (1979). Improving policing: A problem-oriented approach. *Journal of Research in Crime and Delinquency*, 25(2), 236-258.

Gould, P., & White, R. (1974). *Mental maps.* New York: Penguin Books.

Granovetter, M. (1973). The Strength of Weak Ties. *American Journal of Sociology*, 78 (May), 1360-1380.

Harries, K. D. (1974). *The geography of crime and justice.* New York: McGraw-Hill.

Harries, K. D. (1980). *Crime and the environment.* Springfield, Il.: Charles C. Thomas.

Harries, K. D. (1990). *Geographic factors in policing.* Washington, DC: Police Executive Research Forum

Hughes, E.C. (1984). *The sociological eye.* New Brunswick, NJ: Transaction Books.

Hunter, A. (1978). Symbols of incivility: social disorder and fear of crime in the neighborhoods. Paper presented at the meeting of the American Society of Criminology, Dallas, TX.

Kalish. C. B. (1974). *Crimes and victims: A report on the Dayton-San Jose pilot survey of victimization.* Washington, DC: U.S. Department of Justice.

Kelling, G. L. (1978, April). Police field services and crime: The presumed effects of a capacity. *Crime and Delinquency*, p. 180.

Kelling, G. L., & Stewart. J. K. (1989). Neighborhoods and police: The maintenance of civil authority. *Perspectives on Policing.* Washington, DC: National Institute of Justice.

Larson, R. C. (1975). Approximating the performance of urban emergency service systems. *Operations Research*, 23, 845-868.

Lavrakas, P., et al. (1981). *Factors Relating to Citizen Involvement in Personal, Household and Neighborhood Anti-Crime Measures: Executive Summary.* Washington, DC: National Institute of Justice.

Los Angeles Police Department (1988). "Automated Reporting System Pilot Program." Grant application to the National Institute of Justice, December 12, 1988.

Maltz, M.D. (1977). Crime statistics: A historical perspective. *Crime and Delinquency*, 23(1) 32-40.

Maltz, M. D., & Waldron, S. (1968). A supervisory communication system for the Boston Police Department. In S.I. Cohn (Ed.) *Law Enforcement Science and Technology II.* Chicago: IITRI.

McGehee, L., & Whiteacre, G. M. (1983). Microcomputers for law enforcement. *The Police Chief*, 52 (3). 24-26.

Merry, S. E. (1981). *Urban danger: Life in a neighborhood of strangers.* Philadelphia: Temple University Press.

Metropolitan Washington Council of Governments (1974). *Citizen safety and bus transit: A study of the relationship between personal safety and bus transit usage in the metropolitan Washington area.* Washington, DC: Department of Transportation.

Newman, 0. (1972). *Defensible space: Crime prevention through urban design.* New York: Macmillan.

Niederhoffer, A. (1967). *Behind the shield.- The police in urban society.* -Garden City, NY: Doubleday Books.

Park, R. E., Burgess, E. W., & McKenzie. R. D. (1925). *The city.* Chicago: University of Chicago Press.

Pauly, G. A., McEwen, J. T., & Finch, S. J. (1967). Computer mapping--A new technique in crime analysis. In S. A. Yefsky (Ed.), *Law Enforcement Science and Technology.* New York: Thomson Book Co.

Pierce. G. L., Spaar, S. A., & Briggs. L. R. (1984). *The character of police work: Implications for the delivery of services.* Boston, MA: Center for Applied Social Research, Northeastern University.

Piore, M.J., & Sabel, C. F. (1984). *The second industrial divide: Possibilities for prosperity.* New York: Basic Books.

Police and computer team up to head off criminals. (1981, May). *The Police Chief*, 48(5), 57.

Porter, T. M. (1986). *The rise of statistical thinking 1820-1900.* Princeton, NJ: Princeton

University Press.

Pyle, G. F., et al. (1974). *The spatial dynamics of crime.* Chicago: University of Chicago Department of Geography.

Robertson, G. W., & Chang, S. K. (1980). CASS: Crime analysis support system. *The Police Chief,* 47 (8) 41-43.

Rumbaut, R. G., & Bittner, E. (1979). Changing conceptions of the police role: A sociological review. In N. Morris and M. Tonry (Eds.), *Crime and Justice: An Annual Review of Research* (Vol. I), pp.239-288. Chicago: University of Chicago.

Sabel, C. F. (1982). *Work and politics.* Cambridge: Cambridge University Press.

Sanders, W.B. (1977). *Detective work: A study of criminal investigations.* New York: Free Press.

Savage, J. (1978). Project FULCIRAN: Computer assistance in crime solutions. FBI *Law Enforcement Bulletin.* 5(8) 9-11.

Shaw, C. R., &McKay, H. D. (1931). *Social factors in juvenile delinquency.* Washington, DC: U.S. Government Printing Office.

Shaw, C. R., & McKay, H. D. (1969). *Juvenile delinquency and urban areas: A study of rates of delinquency in relation to differential characteristics of local communities in American cities.* Chicago: University of Chicago Press. (Original work published 1942)

Sherman, L. W. (1987). Repeat calls to police in Minneapolis. Washington, DC: Crime Control Institute.

Sherman, L. W., Gartin, P. R., & Buerger, M. E. (1989). Hot spots of predatory crime: routine activities and the criminology of place. *Criminology,* 27, 27-56.

E. A. Shils (1975). *Center and periphery: Essays in macrosociology.* Chicago: University of Chicago Press.

Skogan, W. G., & Maxfield, M. G. (1981). *Coping with crime Individual and neighborhood reactions.* Beverly Hills, CA: Sage Publications.

Skolnick, J. (1966) *Justice without trial.* New York: Wiley.

Springer, L. (1974). Crime reception and response behavior: Two views of a Seattle community. " Pennsylvania State University, PhD dissertation.

Stigler. S. M. (1986). *The history of statistics: Vie measurement of uncertainty before 1900.* Cambridge, MA: Belknap.

Stinchcombe, A. S. (in press). Organizations as information processing systems.

Taub, R., Taylor, D. G., & Dunham, J. (1984). *Paths of neighborhood change.* Chicago: University of Chicago Press.

Taylor, R. B., Gottfredson, S. D., & Brower, S. (1985). Attachment to place: Discriminant validity and impacts of disorder on diversity. *American Journal on Community Psychology,* 13(5),525-542.

Taylor, R. B., Shumaker, S. A., & Gottfredson, S. D. (1985). Neighborhood -level links between physical features and local sentiments: Deterioration, fear of crime, and confidence. *Journal of Architectural Planning Research,* 2, 261-275.

Thomson, D. R. (1987). *Intensive probation supervision in Illinois: A first year progress report on the evaluation.* Chicago: Center for Research in Law and Justice, University of Illinois at Chicago.

Tukey, J. W. (1977). *Exploratory data analysis.* Reading, MA: Addison-Wesley.

Turner, A. G. (1972). *The San Jose methods test of known crime victims.* Washington, DC: National Institute of Law Enforcement and Criminal Justice.

Wachs, M. (1989, June 30). U.S. transit subsidy policy: In need of reform. *Science,* pp. 1545-1549.

Waldrop, M.M. (1989, June 30). Who's Minding the Cockpit? *Science,* p. 1533.

Walsh, J. P. (1988). Organizational change and the division Of labor: The effects of "super-marketism" on the organization of work. Paper presented at the American Sociological Association annual meeting, Atlanta, GA.

Williams, R. (1986, January). Computerized crime map spots crime patterns. *Law and Order,* pp.

28-31.

Wilson, J. Q. (1968). *Varieties of police behavior*. Cambridge, MA: Harvard University Press.

Wilson, J. Q. (1975). *Thinking about crime*. New York: Basic Books.

Wilson, J. Q., & Herrnstein, R. J. (1985). *Crime and human nature*. New York: Simon and Schuster.

Wilson, J. Q.. & Kelling, G. (1982, March). Broken windows: The police and neighborhood safety. *Atlantic Monthly*. pp. 29-38.

Index

0 1341 1825009 8

CPSIA information can be obtained
at www.ICGtesting.com
Printed in the USA
LVHW081506301019
635836LV00005B/212/P

9 781376 261288